# UNLOCKING
# GEOGRAPHY
# SKILLS
# AND
# CONCEPTS

Robert M. Goldberg and Richard M. Haynes

**Globe Book Company**
New York/Cleveland/Toronto

# ABOUT THE AUTHORS

**Robert M. Goldberg** holds a B.A. from Brooklyn College, an M.A. from New York University, and a professional certificate in administration and supervision from Queens College. He is a social studies specialist, active in the fields of urban education, remedial teaching, geography, citizenship education, and also in the development of techniques for teaching social studies skills. Mr. Goldberg is a member of the National Council for the Social Studies, New York State Association for Supervision and Curriculum Development, and the Long Island Council of Social Studies. He was formerly educational consultant for Diagnostic, Prescriptive, and Remediation Teaching in Oceanside, New York. He is currently chairman of the social studies department as well as facilitator for the special education teachers and other teams of teachers interested in interdisciplinary approaches to teaching at Oceanside Middle School. In addition to this book, Mr. Goldberg is coauthor of Globe's *Unlocking Social Studies Skills, Exploring Ameri-* *can Citizenship, Unlocking the Constitution and the Declaration of Independence,* and *Exploring the Urban World.*

**Richard M. Haynes** holds a B.S. from Florida Southern College, an M.A.T. from Rollins College, and an Ed.D. from Duke University. He is a social studies specialist, active in the field of reading and writing remediation and especially interested in southern history. Dr. Haynes is a member of the National Council for the Social Studies and the Association for Supervision and Curriculum Development. Dr. Haynes was formerly Secondary Coordinator of Social Studies and Languages for Durham County School System. He is currently Assistant Superintendent of Instruction for the Tarboro City Schools, Tarboro, North Carolina. In addition to this book, Dr. Haynes is coauthor of Globe's *Unlocking the Constitution and the Declaration of Independence.*

# CONSULTANTS

Pat Diggs, Social Studies Teacher, Palo Duro High School, Amarillo, Texas

David A. Lanegran, Professor, Department of Geography, Macalester College, Saint Paul, Minnesota

Ira Zornberg, Assistant Principal, Social Studies, Thomas Jefferson High School, New York City Public Schools

**Editorial Director:** Richard G. Gallin
**Editor:** Joan Horyczun and PC&F, Inc.
**Photo Editor:** Adelaide Garvin Ungerland
**Cover and Text Designs:** Arthur Ritter
**Project Development, Production, and Technical Illustration:** PC&F, Inc.

**Creative Illustrations:** Dave Blanchette, pgs. 2, 6, 15, 23, 29, 36, 41, 75, 90, 94, 101; Walter Fournier, pgs. 10, 14, 48, 81, 83, 106, 107.

**Photograph Acknowledgments:** pg. 3, Beryl Goldberg; pg. 7, Taurus Photos; pg. 8, NOAA; pg. 19, NOAA; pg. 31 (top left), (Joe Munroe) Photo Researchers, Inc.; pg. 31 (top right), Photo Researchers, Inc.; pg. 31 (bottom left), (Louis Borie) Visuals Unlimited; pg. 31 (bottom right), S.A. Tourism Board; pg. 32 (left), H. Armstrong Roberts; pg. 32 (right), TASS from Sovfoto; pg. 43 (left), (Enell, Inc.) Frederick Lewis; pg. 43 (right), (Abrit Images) Gamma Liaison Agency; pg. 57 (top), (Charles Marden Fitch) Taurus Photos; pg. 57 (bottom left), (J. Ph. Charbonnier) Photo Researchers, Inc.; pg. 57 (bottom right), (Toni Angermayer) Photo Researchers, Inc.; pg. 59, (Lynn Lennon) Photo Researchers, Inc.; pg. 67 (top left), (Mac's Foto) Photo Researchers, Inc.; pg. 67 (top right), (Tom Campbell) West Light; pg. 67 (bottom left), Beryl Goldberg; pg. 67 (bottom right), (Rapho) Photo Researchers, Inc.; pg. 68, (Martin Helfer) Shostal Associates; pg. 73, (Jacques Pavlovski) Sygma; pg. 76, Culver Pictures, Inc.; pg. 90, (Stuart Franklin) Sygma; pg. 97 (left), Beryl Goldberg; pg. 97 (right), (Rene Burri) Magnum; pg. 102 (left), (Georg Gerster) Photo Researchers, Inc.; pg. 102 (middle), (Frederick Lewis) American Stock Photos; pg. 102 (right), (Fritz Henle) Photo Researchers, Inc.

ISBN: 0-87065-895-6

# Contents

# Skills and Concepts

## Skills

The list indicates exercises in which the skills are developed or used.

Vocabulary Skills   Knowing New Words, 1, 6, 10, 15, 23, 29, 36, 41, 48, 51, 56, 66, 71, 75, 80, 89, 94, 100;   Building Your Vocabulary, 4, 21, 33, 45, 85

Comprehension Skills   Using What You Know (includes Unit Reviews), 21–22, 45–47, 62–65, 85–88, 93, 98;   Understanding What You Have Read, 4–5, 22, 27, 39, 44, 46, 50, 55, 60–61, 69, 78, 103;   Living Your Geography, 64–65;   Thinking with Geography, 39;   Reviewing the Facts, 2–3, 7–8, 11–12, 16–18, 24–27, 30–32, 37–39, 42–43, 49–50, 53–54, 58–60, 68–69, 72–73, 76–77, 81–82, 90–91, 95–96, 101–102

Visual Skills   Interpreting Cartoons, 2, 6, 15, 23–24, 29–30, 36–37, 41, 48–49, 75, 81, 83, 90, 94–95, 100–101;   Interpreting Charts, 43, 57, 65, 78, 86–87, 99;   Interpreting Diagrams, 42, 51, 56;   Interpreting Photos, 7, 8, 31, 32, 57, 67, 97;   Interpreting Pictographs, 80–81; Interpreting Puzzles, 71–72

Writing Skills   55, 79, 80, 83, 84;   Writing and Thinking, 2, 6–7, 10–11, 15–16, 23–24, 29–30, 36–37, 41, 48–49, 51–53, 57, 66–67, 71–72, 75, 80–81, 89–90, 94–95, 100–101, 104–105;   Writing an Essay, 70, 103

Analytic Skills   5;   Categorizing, 74;   Classifying, 103;   Comparing, 8–9;   Critical Thinking, 69, 78, 86–87;   Distinguishing True and False Statements, 27, 55, 91–92, 97;   Getting the Main Idea, 80–81, 83, 105–106;   Making Inferences, 64, 70, 86–87;   Outlining, 61;   Reading for a Purpose, 1, 6, 10, 15, 23, 29, 36, 41, 48, 51, 56, 66, 71, 75, 80, 89, 94, 100, 107

Map Skills   Completing and Making Maps, 14, 55;   Reading, Interpreting, and Understanding Maps, 2–3, 7, 8–9, 10–11, 12, 13, 17–18, 23–24, 25–26, 39, 47, 51–53, 62–63, 87–88, 92–93, 104–105, 108–123

Using Maps   Climate, 62–63;   Directions, 9, 13;   Identifying Continents, 28;   Identifying Landforms and Waterforms, 35;   Identifying Map Projections, 25–27, 28;   Identifying Places, 18, 22, 47;   Latitude and Longitude, 19–20, 22, 57–60;   Locating Places, 9; Topography, 34, 47

## Concepts

**Chapter 1:** geography, globe, map   **Chapter 2:** chart, chartographer, compass rose   **Chapter 3:** legend or key, scale   **Chapter 4:** latitude, longitude   **Chapter 5:** map distortion, map projections, (conic, cylinder, plane) hemispheres   **Chapter 6:** landforms, population location   **Chapter 7:** effects of earth's spinning on ocean currents and airflow   **Chapter 8:** source of rainfall, river formation   **Chapter 9:** climate and its effects on people   **Chapter 10:** factors that affect climate   **Chapter 11:** climate zones based on latitude, climate's effect on population location   **Chapter 12:** culture, basic human needs, technology and environment, geographical location and spread of culture, ethnocentrism   **Chapter 13:** natural resources   **Chapter 14:** cities and their origin, people's response to natural environment   **Chapter 15:** effects of technology, Industrial Revolution   **Chapter 16:** value of natural resources   **Chapter 17:** cultural diffusion, interdependence, world political divisions   **Chapter 18:** physical and cultural regions, adaptation to regions, urbanization

*Chapter* **1**

# What Is Geography?

## Reading for a Purpose

1. What is geography?
2. Why is geography important to you?
3. What is a geographer?

## Knowing New Words

**geography** (jee-OG-ruh-fee)   The study of the face of the earth, its climate, its space, and what it has to meet people's needs. The features of an area.
Tim found out that the **geography** of the country was harsh.

**geographer** (jee-OG-ruh-fur)   Someone who studies geography.
The **geographer** learned of the rugged land and the lack of a main water source.

**surface** (SUR-fis)   The top, or face, of something.
One thing that a geographer studies is the **surface** of the earth.

**resources** (REE-sohrs-is)   What a place has that meets people's needs.
Food and water are basic **resources** that everyone needs.

**climate** (KLY-mit)   The average weather in a place over a long period of time.
Her home state's **climate** consists of hot summers and very cold winters with rainfall that comes chiefly in spring and summer.

**Geography** is the study of many things. It is the study of the **surface**, or face, of the earth. It is the study of the **climate** and of the things, or **resources**, an area has to meet people's needs. Geography is also the study of the relationship between people and the places in which they live. A person who studies geography is called a **geographer.** Two main tools of a geographer are maps and globes.

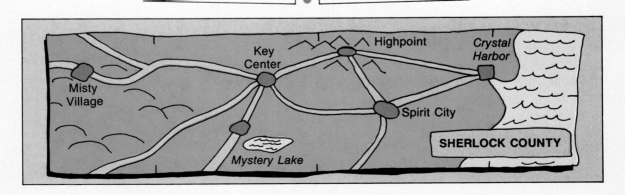

## Writing and Thinking

Study the cartoon carefully. Then answer the questions that follow.

1. What do you think geography is?

   _____

   _____

   _____

2. What things do you think make up geography?

   _____

   _____

   _____

3. What do you think you might learn from studying geography?

   _____

   _____

4. Why do you think that studying geography might be important?

   _____

   _____

● After reading this chapter, come back to the Writing and Thinking activity. Make any changes that you think will make your answers better.

# Geography Skills and Concepts

1.  Imagine that you awakened one morning in a world where there were no maps and globes. You would turn on the TV and there would be no weather map. There would be no news from around the world. Soon food would disappear from the grocery shelves. Trucks could not bring things from farms to market without any road maps. The trucks could not run because oil, which is turned into gas, could not be found without maps. Planes could not fly and ships could not sail. Our way of life would stop.

2.  You can see that maps and globes are very important to all of us. They are used to help us understand geography, which tells us a lot about the earth we live on. We all use geography many times each day without thinking about it.

3.  A globe is a small model of the earth. Globes show the surface of the earth, the land, and the oceans. But with a globe you can only see a part of the earth's surface at one time because part of it is always facing away from you.

2

4. Maps are flat drawings that show all or any part of the earth. Maps can be used for special reasons, such as to show weather as it moves toward you, or to tell drivers how to get from one place to another. Maps can be drawn to show special information, such as where oil might be found. There are thousands of uses for maps that allow us to live the way we do.

5. Geography is the study of the earth and the people who live on it. There are five ways to study the geography of the earth.
   a. Surface. The study of the surface of the earth includes the many forms of the land and the way each form affects the people who live on it.
   b. Climate. The study of the earth's climate includes such things as temperature, rainfall, winds, and seasons. Weather has a lot to do with how people live in a particular place.
   c. Resources. Geography includes a study of the resources of a particular place, or what the place supplies to meet people's needs. Is the soil good for growing crops? Are there fish or good grazing lands for farm animals? Are there forests or minerals of value? Is there enough water?
   d. Space. The study of an area's space includes its size and the land on which people live.
   e. People. The study of people includes not only who lives in a particular area but also how they make a living, what they have learned, and what they are like.

6. Geography is about the relationship of the earth and its people. It is the study of an area's resources and how people change to take advantage of these resources. The study of geography is important because it helps you to understand and use the world in which you live; it also makes possible your lifestyle, or the way you live in the world.

*What are the advantages and disadvantages of using a globe rather than a map?*

## Building Your Vocabulary

Complete each of the following sentences. Then find and circle the words in the puzzle. The hidden words may be spelled from top to bottom, bottom to top, left to right, right to left, and diagonally. Circle the words as you find them.

1. Someone who studies geography is a _____.

2. The face of the earth is called the _____.

3. A small model of the eath is a _____.

4. A flat drawing that shows all or any part of the earth is a _____.

5. Such things as temperature, rainfall, winds, and seasons are part of the study of

_____.

6. The things a place supplies to meet people's needs are known as _____.

7. An area's size and the land on which people live is _____.

8. The study of the face of the earth and the people who live on it is called

_____.

```
W   Z   S   Y   E   L   P   O   E   P   T   O   D
G   B   G   C   L   O   M   Q   M   R   J   C   Y
X   I   D   E   P   Q   A   E   A   O   T   L   S
V   R   K   O   O   T   M   G   P   E   P   I   N
N   E   R   N   W   G   D   A   L   E   U   M   X
F   S   X   S   L   I   R   Z   Y   O   H   A   G
S   O   J   C   M   O   X   A   P   Y   B   T   U
S   U   R   F   A   C   E   S   P   Z   O   E   P
W   R   V   R   Y   T   A   Q   B   H   B   I   L
U   C   L   Z   G   I   V   C   O   S   E   H   G
G   E   T   R   O   S   P   A   C   E   A   R   D
A   S   J   Q   H   N   Z   C   E   T   S   M   U
X   U   T   S   Y   H   P   A   R   G   O   E   G
```

## Understanding What You Have Read

1. List the maps that you have seen today or that you know you will see. Tell what each map is for.

_____

_____

**2.** There are five parts to the study of geography. List each one, tell what it is, and give an example of how that part of geography affects your life.

| Part of Geography | What It Is | Example from My Life |
| --- | --- | --- |
| _____ | _____ | _____ |
| _____ | _____ | _____ |
| _____ | _____ | _____ |
| _____ | _____ | _____ |
| _____ | _____ | _____ |

● If you have not already done so, go back to your answers to the Writing and Thinking Activity on page 2. Make any changes that would make your answers better.

# GEOGRAPHY HIGHLIGHTS

## World Population

■ What is the world's population? The question is impossible to answer. People are being born and people are dying every minute of the day. Also, some countries do not try to keep count of how many people they have. The United States counts the number of people in the country once every 10 years. That count is called a census (SEN-sus). We do know about how many people there are on earth—about 5 billion (5,000,000,000). The United States has about 240,000,000 people. That is about 5 percent of the world's population today.

# Chapter 2

# What Are Maps?

## Reading for a Purpose

1. What is cartography?
2. How are satellite pictures and maps alike and different?
3. How can you tell direction on a map?

## Knowing New Words

**cartographer** (kar-TOG-ruh-fur)   A skilled person who draws maps.
My friend's mother was an expert **cartographer**.

**direction** (dih-REK-shun)   The relationship of one place to another.
I found out that north was the **direction** in which I wanted to go.

**compass rose** (KUM-pus ROHZ)   A symbol that shows direction on a map.
The **compass rose** on the map showed that we should go northwest.

**satellite** (SAT-uh-lyt)   An object sent into space to go around the earth or other body.
The picture was taken from a **satellite**.

Is there a difference between a satellite picture of the earth, a picture taken from above earth, and a map? In some ways they are alike, but there are important differences between them. A **compass rose** to help you tell **direction** is found on most maps, but not on a **satellite** photo.

## Writing and Thinking

Read and study the cartoon carefully. Then answer the questions on page 7.

1. What are two ways to show what a state looks like on paper?

_____

_____

2. List three ways you think a map might be different from a photograph taken from space?

_____

_____

3. Which would you rather travel with, a satellite photo or a map? Explain your answer.

_____

_____

4. What do you think the clerk will tell the man? Write your answer in the "bubble" in which she is speaking.

5. Are maps just like satellite photos? Explain your answer.

_____

_____

● After reading this chapter, come back to the answers you have written. Make any changes that you think will make your answers better.

## Geography Skills and Concepts

1. Imagine being the first person to find a new land and being asked to draw a map of what it looked like. Soon after America was first discovered that is what some people were asked to do. A person who draws maps is very skilled, and he or she is called a **cartographer**. The process of drawing a map is called *cartography*. The first maps of the New World, as America was called then, were only rough guesses of what the area really looked like. But as more and more cartographers studied America, the maps got better and better. An outline map of America today looks as if a satellite camera took a picture of it because it is so correctly drawn.

2. When a map is being made, the cartographer has many things to do. The first step is to draw an accurate outline of the area, showing it just as it would look from space. Today this is usually done by using a satellite photo of the area being drawn. The photo is taken from many miles in space so that it shows exactly how the area looks from above. Since shapes and outlines are shown exactly as they are, these photos help the cartographer to draw accurate maps.

*This satellite photograph shows the area from the Mediterranean Sea to Antarctica.*

3. The next step in making a map is deciding what information to put on it. Maps can show many things. A map may show and label rivers, highways, towns, and areas of interest. The information put on a map depends on the purpose for which the map will be used. Cartographers draw land areas or areas of water. When a land area, such as a state, is drawn, it is called a map. Drivers need maps to help them go from one place to another. When an area of water, such as an ocean, is drawn, it is called a chart. Charts are often used by sea captains to guide ships from one port to another.

4. An important feature on both a map and a chart is the way to tell direction. To tell direction we use a compass. The needle of a compass faces north. The other main directions, or points, of a compass are east, south, and west. The compass on a map or chart shows the major directions; it is called a compass rose. You will almost never see a map that doesn't have a compass rose on it because such a map would be of little value. With a compass rose you can tell that one thing is north of another, or to the east, and so on. The first letter of the points of a compass, N, S, E, and W, can be arranged to make a word. Do you know what it is? If a place is halfway between two directions, say north and east, it is called northeast. Other such directions are southeast, southwest, and northwest.

## Comparing a Map and a Satellite Photograph

Study the map and the satellite photograph of South Florida. Then check the column that shows which you would use, the map or the photograph, to find the following features. For some features, you may check both columns.

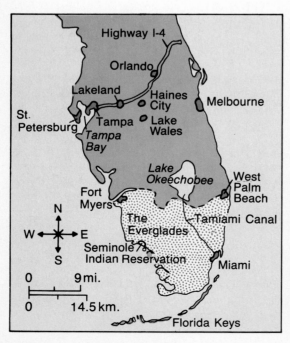

| Feature | Map | Photograph |
|---|---|---|
| 1. shows an outline of South Florida | _____ | _____ |
| 2. shows Tampa Bay | _____ | _____ |
| 3. names Tampa Bay | _____ | _____ |
| 4. shows where Orlando is | _____ | _____ |
| 5. can be used to find the Everglades | _____ | _____ |
| 6. shows the Florida Keys | _____ | _____ |
| 7. shows the Tamiami Canal | _____ | _____ |
| 8. shows direction | _____ | _____ |
| 9. names the towns | _____ | _____ |
| 10. shows an American Indian (Native American) reservation | _____ | _____ |

## Locating Places

Study the map and the satellite photo of South Florida on page 8. Find each feature listed below on the map. Then find and number each feature on the satellite photo.

1. Lakeland
2. Tampa
3. Highway I-4
4. Lake Okeechobee
5. The Everglades
6. A port

## Using Directions

Locate the cities listed below on the map on page 8. For each, write the direction of the second city from the first. For example, to go from Tampa to St. Petersburg you would go in a southwest direction.

1. To go from St Petersburg to Tampa, you would go in a _____ direction.
2. To go from Haines City to Lake Wales, you would go in a _____ direction.
3. To go from Fort Myers to West Palm Beach, you would go in a _____ direction.
4. To go from West Palm Beach to Miami, you would go in a _____ direction.
5. To go from Miami to Tampa, you would go in a _____ direction.
6. To go from Tampa to Melbourne, you would go in a _____ direction.
7. To go from Melbourne to Fort Myers, you would go in a _____ direction.
8. To go from Fort Myers to Lakeland, you would go in a _____ direction.
9. To go from Lakeland to West Palm Beach, you would go in a _____ direction.
10. To go from West Palm Beach to Fort Myers, you would go in a _____ direction.

# Chapter **3**

## How Can You Learn to Use Maps?

### Reading for a Purpose

1. What is a map key, or legend?
2. How can you use a map to find your way?
3. How can you tell distance on a map?

### Knowing New Words

**symbols** (SIM-buls)   A drawing, or figure, that stands for something.
   Susan pointed out that the stars on the map were the **symbols** for state capitals.

**legend** (LEJ-und)   The explanation of what colors and symbols mean on a map.
   Henry used the map **legend** to find the symbol for the state capital.

**map scale** (MAP SKAYL)   Compares the distance on a map to the distance of a place on earth.
   André said that on this **map scale** one inch equals 50 miles.

People have used maps for hundreds of years to help them get from one place to another. But how can drawings on paper tell you where you are going? Or how far you will go? How can a map tell you about the things you will see along the way? This chapter will tell you how to use a map to find your way.

### Writing and Thinking

Below is a map that Fighting Eagle drew to show the hunters in his village where to find deer. Study his map; then answer the questions on page 11.

1. Does Fighting Eagle want the hunters to go toward the sun or not? Explain your answer.

_____

_____

_____

2. Could the hunters get wet as they head for the deer? Explain your answer.

_____

_____

3. Can you tell how far the hunters will have to go to find the deer? Explain your answer.

_____

_____

4. What two things could you add to make this map more useful?

_____

_____

● After reading this chapter, come back to the answers you have written. Make any changes that you think will make your answers better.

## Geography Skills and Concepts

1. A map is not just a picture of the earth or some small part of it. Like this book, a map is a tool that can be read, studied, and learned from. The cartographer who draws a map puts in features to help the reader. A **legend** is used to explain what each of the **symbols** on the map means. The cartographer also uses a **map scale** and a compass rose to help the reader.

2. Fighting Eagle's map is easy to read because the symbols he used are simple. When a map is going to be used to show many features, the legend becomes more difficult. Here is a legend from a road map. This legend shows many symbols.

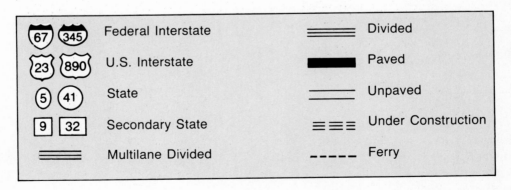

3. You can learn many things about roads by studying the legend. The legend shows you different types of roads, from the best and fastest roads, which are called multilane, to divided highways and plain dirt roads. It also shows you "superhighways," which are roads that go from state to state.

These are called interstate highways. The legend also shows "secondary roads," which are less traveled and are the slowest to drive on. It tells you which roads were built by the federal government, "U.S. highways," and which were built by the state, "state highways." The legend even shows you which roads have not been finished and where you might have to take a ferryboat between roads.

4. Another important feature on a map is direction. The map shows direction by the compass rose. It tells in which direction north, south, east, and west are. If you look at the map that Fighting Eagle drew, you will see that no direction was shown on it other than his use of the sun. That map was of use only while the sun stayed where it was. A road map, as well as other maps, can be used at any time because directions do not change.

5. Use the map legend to trace the most direct path you would take to travel from Cleveland, Ohio, to Detroit, Michigan. You will also want to travel on good roads.
   Follow this path on the road map below.
   a. Find Cleveland, Ohio, on the map.
   b. Then take Interstate 80 to U.S. Highway 250.
   c. Go north on U.S. Highway 250 to Sandusky. The ferry will take you north to near Leamington, Canada.
   d. Then take state road 3 to Detroit.

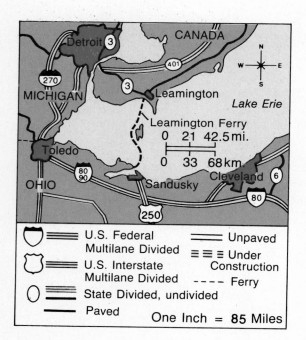

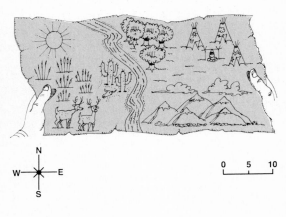

6. How far have you gone on your trip? This road map tells you the scale of miles. A map scale compares the distance on a map to the distance between places on earth. Every inch on the map above is equal to 85 miles on the earth's surface. That means that two inches on the map is equal to 170 miles (2 × 85). How many miles would one-half inch equal?

7. Look at this second map of Fighting Eagle's. A compass rose has been added to the map. You can now see that the deer are southwest of the village. Are the mountains south of the village? The second map also has a scale of miles. Can you tell how far away the deer are?

## Using Directions

Study this road map of Massachusetts. You are to take a trip from Sagamore in the east to Adams in the west. Complete the directions below the map by using the compass directions such as north, southwest, east, and by using road names. Use the best road you can for each part of the trip.

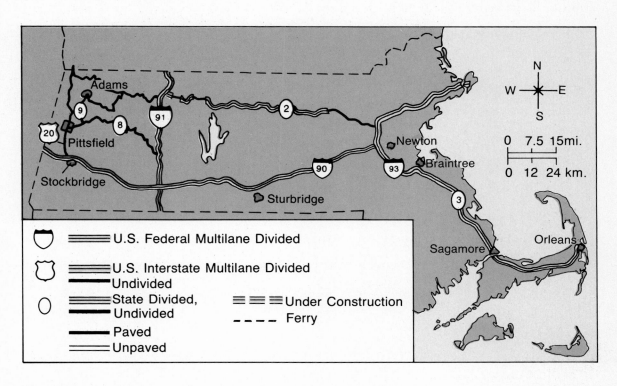

1. From Sagamore go _____ on route _____.

2. Near Braintree turn _____ on route _____.

3. Just north of Newton, turn _____ on _____.

4. The road you picked up near Newton is a _____ type of road.

5. Continue going _____ on _____ to near Stock-bridge.

6. Near Stockbridge turn _____ on route _____.

7. This road is a _____ type of road.

8. At Pittsfield, turn _____ on _____, going a short distance.

9. Look for _____ going _____ to Adams.

10. Using the scale of miles, on a straight line how far did this trip take you? _____

11. Can you find another route to Adams? List the roads that you would take to follow this route.

_____

_____

13

## Completing a Map

On the outline map below draw the route you would follow to find the hidden treasure. The steps that you are to follow are listed here. Use the compass rose and the scale of miles to help you draw the route. You may have to draw in other details (for example, the cliff) besides the route to make the route clearer. Draw the map so that others can follow your route to find the treasure. Be sure to put a legend on the map to explain the symbols you added.

1. You start at the old oak tree near the fence and go north one mile to the lake.

2. At the lake you go east $\frac{1}{2}$ mile to the cliff. Follow the cliff south to the marsh.

3. Walk through the marsh to the northeast $1\frac{1}{4}$ miles to the path.

4. The path goes northeast two miles to the river, which flows from the north to the marsh.

5. Go north along the river $\frac{1}{2}$ mile to the bridge. The bridge crosses from east to west.

6. The road that uses the bridge goes from Westport on the west seven miles to Goldberg. Take the road two miles toward Westport. There you will find the old Indian path going north and south.

7. Take the path south $\frac{1}{4}$ mile to the bend, which goes west. In the bend keep going south another $\frac{1}{4}$ mile to the hanging oak tree. Others who tried to find the treasure found out how the oak tree got that name. The treasure is buried to the west of the oak tree at its base.

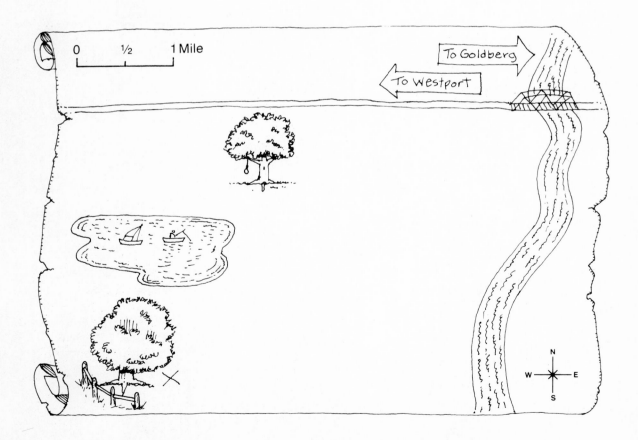

# Chapter 4

# How to Locate Places on a Map

## Reading for a Purpose

1. How can you find places on a map?
2. How can latitude and longitude help you find your way?
3. How can a special system of lines called a grid help you find places on a map?

## Knowing New Words

**equator** (ih-KWAY-tur)   The line of latitude exactly halfway between the North Pole and the South Pole.
> Life at the **equator** can be very hot and steamy.

**latitude** (LAT-ih-tood)   A distance north or south of the equator.
> They found life hard, living in the high **latitudes**.

**longitude** (LON-jih-tood)   Distance east or west on the earth.
> As Donna flew west, she changed **longitude** by 10 degrees.

**meridian** (muh-RID-ee-un)   A line of longitude.
> The first, or prime, line of longitude is called the prime **meridian**; it runs north and south through Greenwich, England.

**location** (loh-KAY-shun)   A position on the earth's surface.
> To find a **location**, both latitude and longitude are used.

How can you locate a place on a map? There is a system of measuring that can help you to find places quickly and easily on maps and globes. This means of measuring is called latitude and longitude. If you know how to use this system, you can quickly locate any place on earth.

## Writing and Thinking

Study the cartoon carefully. Then answer the questions on page 16.

Use the cartoon on page 15 to answer the questions.

1. What would help you to find a location on a map or a globe?

_____

_____

2. How many measurements do you need to find a location on a map or globe?

_____

3. Which person would you rather fly with? Why did you choose that person?

_____

_____

4. What do you think that "30°N, 90°W" stands for?

_____

_____

● After reading this chapter, come back to the answers you have written. Make any changes that you think will make your answers better.

# Geography Skills and Concepts

1. Imagine that you are a sea captain sailing across the ocean from Seattle, Washington, to Honolulu, Hawaii. You know that there are no road signs or places where you can stop and ask for directions along the way. One small mistake in direction and you will not be able to locate the Hawaiian islands. Thousands of miles of open ocean would be in every direction. How can you figure out how to sail directly to Honolulu? You learned in Chapter 2 that a map shows land areas and a chart shows water areas. As captain, you should use your charts. As with maps and globes, charts also show **latitude** and **longitude**.

2. Latitude is used to measure the distance from the middle of the earth to either pole. As you can see on the globe, lines of latitude run east and west around the earth. The line around the middle of the earth is called the **equator**. The root word *equal* is part of **equator**. It is an equal distance from the equator to either pole. The lines from the equator to the South Pole are called south latitude. The lines between the equator and the North Pole are called north latitude. These lines do not really appear on the earth; they are imaginary. They are only drawn on charts, maps, and globes.

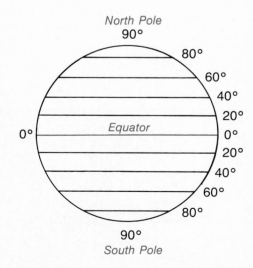

**3.** Latitude is measured in degrees. Degree is shown as "°" when it is written. In the cartoon the people were at 40° north latitude. That can be written as 40°N. There are 90° between the equator and each pole. Degrees are measured away from the equator. The higher the number of degrees, the further away it is from the equator. You know that the North Pole and the South Pole are both very cold. That explains why life in the high latitudes, which are near either pole, is hard and cold.

**4.** To find exactly where a place is, you also need to use longitude. Longitude is used to measure distances east and west on the earth. As you can see on the globe, lines of longitude cut up the globe into sections. Lines of longitude are also measured in degrees.

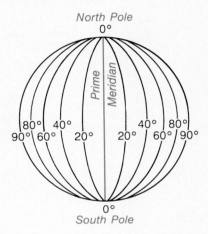

**5.** Another name of a line of longitude is **meridian**. A place had to be picked for the first line of longitude. Greenwich, England, was used. This first line is called the prime meridian. The prime meridian is 0°. Everything to the east of the prime meridian is measured in degrees east, such as 45°E. To the west, everything is shown in degrees west , such as 40°W. There are 180° east from the prime meridian, and 180° west from the prime meridian.

**6.** To find a location, both latitude and longitude are used. Find 40°N on this map of the United States. Follow that line west until you find 75°W; this is between 80° and 70°. In the Writing and Thinking cartoon, you left from Philadelphia, which is at 40°N, 75°W. You flew to 30°N, 90°W. Where did you go?

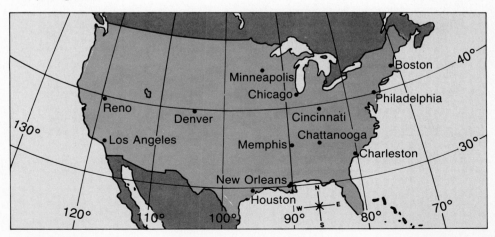

**7.** To figure out how to sail from Hilo, Hawaii, to Honolulu, Hawaii, you will need to know the longitude and latitude of each. Look at the map below. First you must locate the city of Hilo. That is at 19°50′N latitude. This reads "19 degrees, 50 minutes north." Minutes are smaller measurements between degrees. There are 60 minutes in a degree. The longitude of Hilo is 154°60′W. Honolulu is at 21°20′N latitude. The longitude is 157°50′W. So to get from Hilo to Honolulu, you will sail northwest.

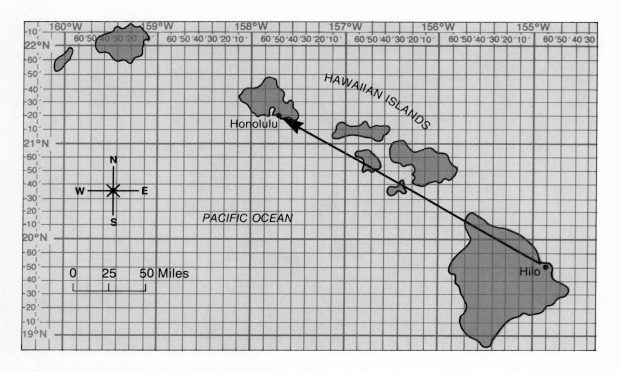

## Identifying Places

On each line write the geographic feature that is being shown.

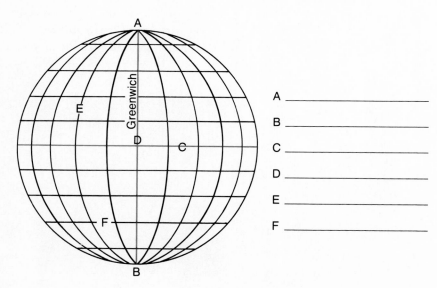

A _____

B _____

C _____

D _____

E _____

F _____

## Using Latitude and Longitude

Hurricane Bob is loose in the Atlantic. See the photograph on page 20. You are being given coordinates (the latitude and longitude of the center of the storm) as the storm moves into the Gulf of Mexico. Mark the path of the storm on the map below so that you can see where it will hit land.

1. Hurricane Bob has crossed the western end of Cuba, going due north to latitude 23°N, longitude 85°W.
2. It slows and turns northwest to 25°N, 88°W.
3. Over warm water Bob gets stronger. He goes north to 27°N, 87°45′. Top winds are traveling 95 miles per hour (mph).
4. Bob drifts toward Louisiana, moving northwest to 28°30′, 89°W. Top winds are traveling 110 mph. New Orleans may be hit.
5. Bob stops and moves very little for 12 hours. Winds: 120 mph.
6. Pensacola, Florida, gets bad news. Bob moves east-northeast at 15 mph. Winds are traveling 125 mph. Bob is plotted at 29°30′N, 86°15′W.
7. Bob turns southeast at the last minute, taking 130 mph winds toward Tampa. Landfall is made at 27°50′N, 82°50′W that evening. Where did Bob hit land?

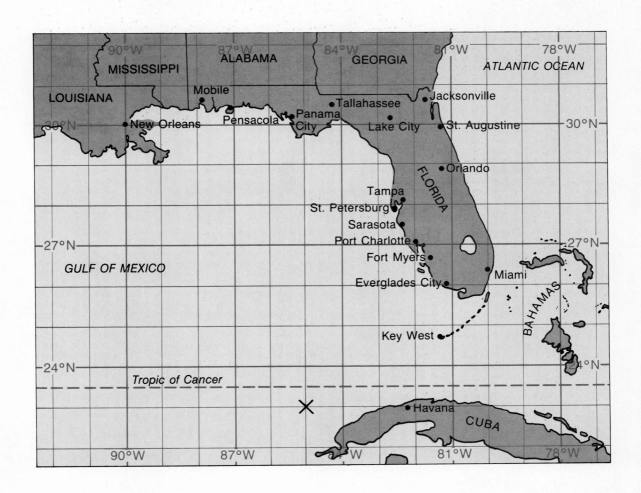

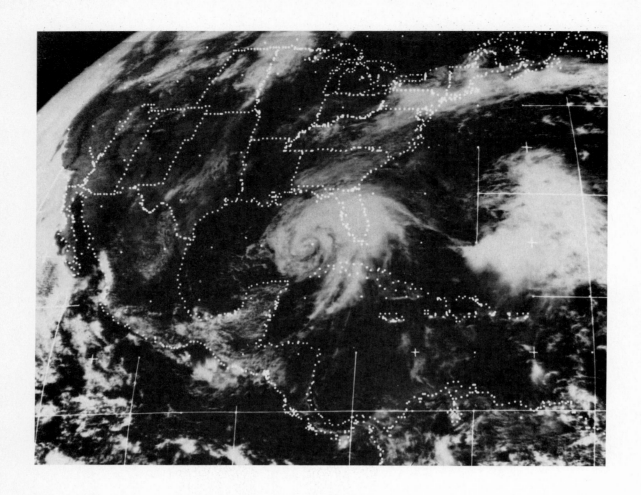

# GEOGRAPHY HIGHLIGHTS

## The International Dateline

■   Where on earth could you go from today into yesterday and into tomorrow all in less than one day? This is a hard question. Where does one day end and another day start for the whole world? There are 360° in a full circle. Half of a circle is 180°. The earth, round like a circle, is divided in half to mark where one day ends and another begins. The starting point, zero, or the prime meridian, is the line of longitude that passes through Greenwich, England. The 180° meridian passes through the Pacific Ocean. This is called the *international dateline,* the place where one day stops and another begins. The dateline zigzags around island groups. To the east of the line it is a day earlier than it is to the west. If you were to cross the international dateline today going west, you'd go from today to yesterday. If you then went east, you would go from what was then today into tomorrow, which is the today you started from! You could go from today to yesterday to tomorrow.

# Unit 1 Review

## Building Your Vocabulary

Complete the crossword puzzle.

**Across**

2. Someone who studies geography.
4. The explanation of what colors and picture symbols are on a map.
5. The line of latitude exactly halfway between the North Pole and the South Pole.
6. A map tool that shows direction.
8. The size of a map compared to the area it shows.
10. A person who draws maps.
12. A drawing or picture that stands for something.
13. What a place offers to meet a person's needs.
14. The relationship of one place to another.

**Down**

1. A line of longitude.
3. The study of the face of the earth, its climate, resources, space, and people.
7. Distance north or south from the equator.
8. The top or face of something.
9. The distance east or west on the globe.
11. The earth's temperature, rainfall, winds, and seasons.

## Identifying Places

On each line write the geographic feature that is being shown.

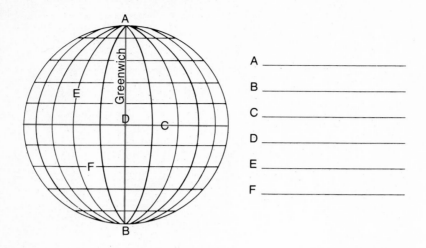

A _____

B _____

C _____

D _____

E _____

F _____

---

## Understanding What You Have Read

Fill in the blanks with the words that best complete each sentence. Choose the best word for each blank from the word bank. The completed sentences can be used as a review of Unit 1.

| | | |
|---|---|---|
| legend | symbols | resources |
| maps | meridians | equator |
| surface | directions | map |
| geography | satellite | geographer |
| cartographer | scale | climate |

The study of _____ includes three things: studying the earth's
(1)

surface, its climate, and its people's needs and resources. Someone who draws maps for a

_____ is called a _____. _____
(2)                                          (3)                          (4)

and globes are the main tools used by people in this field.

A geographer is interested in the earth's _____, which includes the
(5)

land in all of its forms, and its _____, which includes temperature, rainfall,
(6)

winds, and seasons. Geography also includes the earth's _____,
(7)

which is the study of what a place offers to meet its people's needs.

A _____ is a flat drawing of the earth that is not like a
(8)

_____ photograph. A photograph does not have a _____,
(9)                                                              (10)

which explains what colors and pictures mean on a map, a _____, which
(11)

explains distances on a map, or _____, which stand for map features. Also,
(12)

a photograph does not give _____ to find features, or measurements
(13)

of either latitude, which measures distance north or south from the _____,
(14)

or longtitude, which is measured east or west in lines called _____.
(15)

*Chapter* **5**

# Why Are There So Many Kinds of Maps?

## Reading for a Purpose

1. Why are so many kinds of maps needed?
2. What is distortion?
3. What are the names of the continents?
4. How can you tell which kind of map to use?

## Knowing New Words

**distortion** (dih-STOR-shun)   Changing the shape of something.
> Julie said that all maps are a **distortion** of the globe in one way or another.

**continent** (KON-tuh-nunt)   One of the seven largest land masses of the earth.
> Hsing came from the **continent** of Asia.

**hemisphere** (HEM-ih-sfeer)   One-half of the earth.
> The United States is in the Northern **Hemisphere**.

———————•———————

There is no way to make a round surface flat without changing it. To make a map, the rounded surface of the globe must be changed, or distorted, to show it as a flat surface. There are many types of maps. Some maps can show one type of feature without distorting it, but other features must be distorted instead. Each of these maps has a different purpose; each has some **distortion**.

## Writing and Thinking

Study the cartoon carefully. Then answer the questions on page 24.

Use the cartoon on page 23 to answer the questions below.

1. In which way are the three maps in the cartoon alike?

   _____

   _____

2. In which ways is each map different?

   _____

   _____

3. Why do you think there are different kinds of maps?

   _____

   _____

● After reading this chapter, come back to the answers you have written. Make any changes that you think will make your answers better.

# Geography Skills and Concepts

1. Imagine taking an eggshell and trying to flatten it without breaking it. It cannot be done. When a cartographer draws a map of the earth, it is like trying to make the round eggshell flat. When you look at a map of the world, you see it all there on a flat surface. Yet when you look at a globe, you can only see half of the world at a time. How can the cartographer draw the world as if it were flat?

2. There is no way for a cartographer to draw a flat map of the earth and show everything the same way it looks on the globe. The cartographer must decide what to distort, or change, and what features not to distort. Think of it as taking an orange peel that has the **continents**, or large land surfaces, drawn on it like a globe. If you were to cut the orange in half you would have two halves, or **hemispheres**. If the stem of the orange is used as the "North Pole," you would cut the orange into hemispheres at the "equator." That gives you a Northern Hemisphere and a Southern Hemisphere. You can see in the picture that there is a North America and a South America, one in each hemisphere. If you cut the orange "globe" into hemispheres along the prime meridian, you would have an Eastern Hemisphere and a Western Hemisphere.

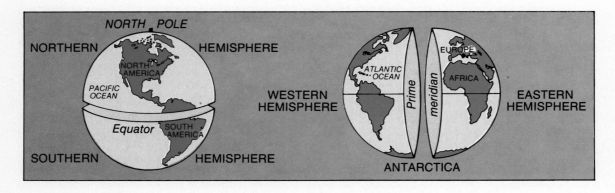

3. Next, imagine trying to flatten each hemisphere into a flat map without changing anything. Since it cannot be done, the cartographer must decide what to distort and what to keep from distorting. This can be done in many ways; that is why there are many different kinds of maps.

4. There are basically three different ways to project, or show, the world as a map. A map projection can be done as (a) a plane, (b) a cone, or (c) a cylinder. Imagine that the globe is an orange and you are peeling it to make it a map. There is no distortion where the map and globe are still touching. The two outer edges are farthest away from the part that still touches the globe. The farther the distance from where they touch, the more the map is distorted. It is like laying an orange peel on a table. Where the orange peel touches the table, there is no stretching to make them meet. When you push the orange peel down on the table to make it flat, the edges of the peel separate. The farther toward the table the peel is pushed, the more it is pulled out of shape, or distorted.

5. Cartographers will distort different features on a map for different reasons. To make the map useful for a particular reason, they try to keep that one feature from being distorted. For example, if you want to compare the shapes of the continents, you would want a map that shows these shapes as they really are. The cartographer would then draw a map that does not distort the shapes. Below are some of the different kinds of map projections. These are two types of world maps. They both show the earth, yet it looks different on each map. The map on the left distorts what the continents look like. But it does not distort the size, or area, of the continents in relation to each other. It is easy to see that the island of Greenland is much smaller than South America. On the map to the right it is easy to find each continent because the shape has stayed the same. But the size of each continent has been changed. Is Greenland still smaller than South America?

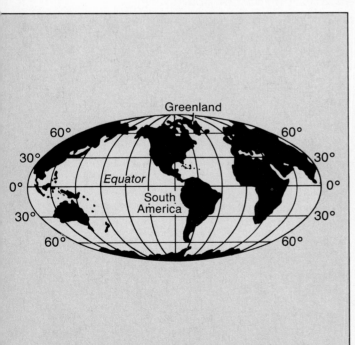

AN EQUAL-AREA MAP PROJECTION

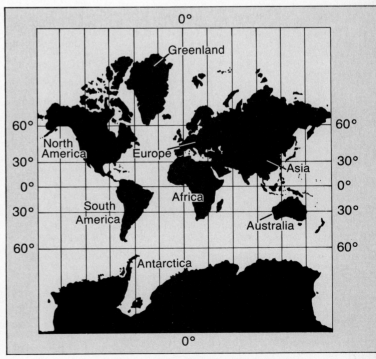

A TRUE-SHAPE MAP PROJECTION

**a.** Below is a type of *cone projection* of the United States. It is a very good projection for showing the United States. There is less distortion on this map because the area being shown is smaller than a map of the entire world. Notice that the lines of latitude are curved on this map. Do they curve the same way on the globe? This happens because of the type of distortion on this map.

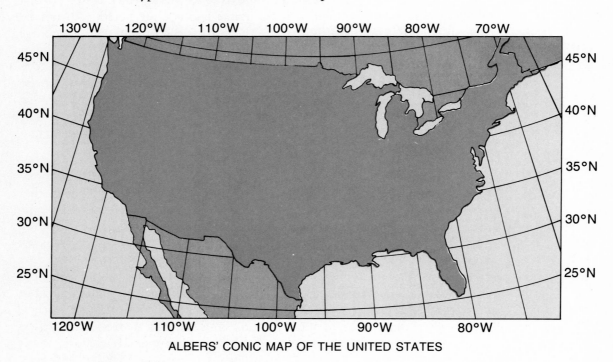

ALBERS' CONIC MAP OF THE UNITED STATES

**b.** Below is a *plane projection*. On this type of map a line drawn with a ruler shows the shortest distance between two points. Draw a line from Washington to Moscow. Look at where the line takes you. This map distorts shape but not the line of travel.

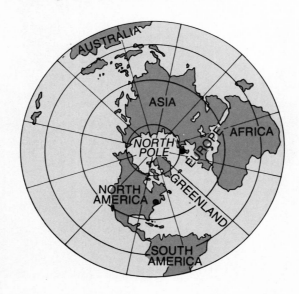

A PLANE PROJECTION CENTERED ON THE NORTH POLE

c. Below is a *cylinder projection*. This type of map is often used in news reports and for classroom maps. It shows each continent's shape without distortion. It shows all compass directions without distortion, too. To make such a good map, other things must be distorted. Is there distortion in the size of Greenland and Africa? Which is distorted?

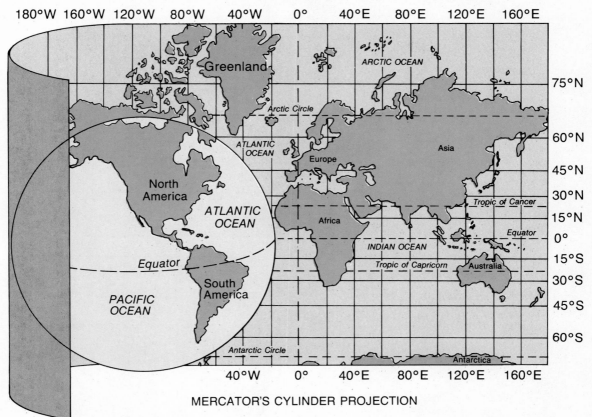

MERCATOR'S CYLINDER PROJECTION

d. There are many kinds of maps because there are many different uses for them, and each use requires a map that does not distort something. There cannot be one perfect map because they are all distorted in one way or another. But there can be a perfect map for a certain use. A good geographer knows how to pick out the right map for each job.

## Understanding What You Have Read

Read each sentence to see if it is true or false. Put a *T* beside each true statement. If the statement is false, put an *F* beside it and rewrite the statement so that it is true.

_____ 1. Distortion happens when a round globe is made to look flat.

_____ 2. A cartographer can draw a world map without distortion.

_____ 3. When drawing a map, a cartographer must decide what to distort and what not to distort.

_____ 4. There is only one way to divide the world into hemispheres—north and south at the equator.

## Identifying Continents

Label each continent on the map.

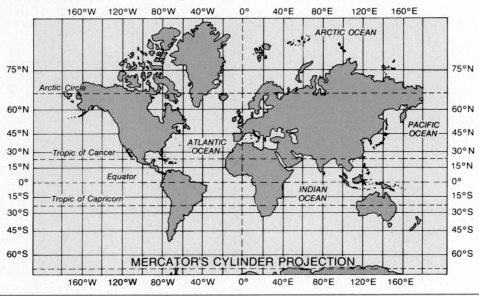

MERCATOR'S CYLINDER PROJECTION

## Identifying Map Projections

Below you will find small maps with different types of distortion. Below the map, write what the cartographer did not distort and what was distorted.

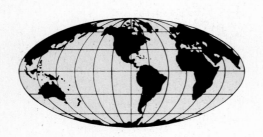

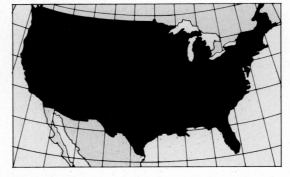

1. distorted: _____

   not distorted: _____

2. distorted: _____

   not distorted: _____

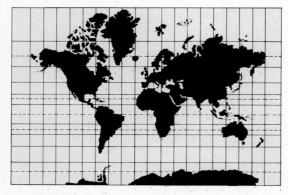

3. distorted: _____

   not distorted: _____

4. distorted: _____

   not distorted: _____

# *Chapter* **6**

## How Are Landforms Mapped?

### Reading for a Purpose

1. What are landforms?
2. How are landforms shown on a map?
3. How do landforms and waterforms affect people?

### Knowing New Words

landforms (LAND-forms)   the types of features found on the earth's surface.
>     As he studied California **landforms**, Bob learned why people live where they do.

topography (tuh-POG-ruh-fee)   The features or landforms on the surface of the earth.
>     Mary is an expert at mapping the **topography** of an area.

environment (en-VY-run-munt)   The conditions in which people live.
>     The upper latitudes provide a harsh **environment**.

adapt (uh-DAPT)   To become used to something.
>     We soon learned to **adapt** to a warm climate.

plateau (plah-TOH)   High, flat land that rises above the ground around it.
>     Arizona has many beautiful **plateaus**.

———————————— ● ————————————

Maps are flat projections of the earth's surface. By using symbols to show different types of land, a map can tell us many things about the earth's surface. It can show the form, or shape, of the land. People who live in a particular area learn to **adapt**, or live with the **landforms** in that area. Landforms help to shape the conditions, or **environment**, in which people live.

### Writing and Thinking

Study the cartoon carefully. Then answer the questions that follow.

29

Use the cartoon on page 29 to answer the questions.

1. What is the man shopping for?

_____

2. What will the man do with what he buys?

_____

3. Are there many kinds of landforms? Name some.

_____

_____

4. Do you think that it is important to show landforms on maps? Explain your answer.

_____

_____

_____

● After reading this chapter, come back to the answers you have written. Make any changes that you think will make your answers better.

## Geography Skills and Concepts

1. As you ride around the town where you live, you probably go up and down some hills. You might see some taller hills or mountains, and maybe a river. Think about the land and its forms—its physical characteristics. You are studying **topography**, which is the shapes and forms of land.

2. Geographers study landforms carefully. Landforms are the types of surface features that are found on the earth's surface. There are many kinds of landforms. Geographers group landforms into four main types:
   a. Plains—flat or almost flat land that is often good for farming.
   b. Hills—rolling land that rises above the land around it.
   c. Mountains—very high, hilly land that rises above the land around it.
   d. Plateaus—high, flat land that rises above the ground around it.

3. A map that shows the surface of the earth is called a topographic map. When reading a topographic map, you should be able to tell what landforms are shown. To put this information on a topographic map, cartographers use symbols.

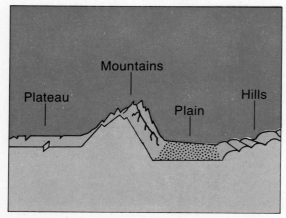

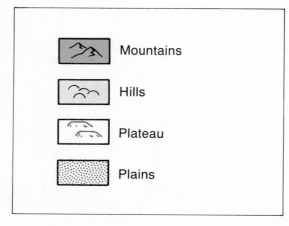

*Why are the best farmlands on the plains?*

*These mountains are part of the Sierra Nevada range in California. What are some industries in mountain regions?*

a. **Plains:** These are a nearly level area. Plains are important to people because they are often the best and easiest lands to farm. They are also easy to travel across and to build on. A damp and muddy plain may be called a swamp. Other plains that are very dry and get little rainfall are known as deserts. Around a desert there may be sand hills or sand dunes.

b. **Hills:** When mountains and plains are near each other, there are usually hills between them. Often rivers and lakes will be found in hilly areas. If the way in which a river flows is important, the map will have an arrow that marks the direction of the flow. When a river is full only when there is a hard rain, it will be marked as a dry riverbed. When the river suddenly falls over rocks, it will be marked as a waterfall. A line of such waterfalls may be marked as a fall line.

c. **Mountains:** When mountains form in a line, they are called a range, or mountain range. The tallest mountains will be shown as peaks. Where there are valleys in the mountains that are easy to pass through, these are called passes. The hills around mountains are called foothills because they are at the foot of the mountains.

d. **Plateaus:** These are level areas raised sharply above the land around them. Sometimes they are called tablelands because they look like giant tabletops on the earth. A plateau with steep sides and a very flat top may also be called a mesa. Where a river has worn a deep cut into a plateau, the opening it creates is called a canyon.

*These hills are in the lake region of South Ontario. Do you think many people live in this region?*

*Table Mountain, shown in the distance, is in South Africa. Why do you think it is called Table Mountain?*

31

**4.** Where the land and water meet is called a coast, seacoast, or coastline. The United States has two main coasts. One faces east on the Atlantic Ocean and is called the East Coast. The other, on the Pacific Ocean, is called the West Coast. There are special landforms where land and water meet. When a narrow strip of land is bordered by water on three sides, it is called a peninsula. When a small piece of land is fully surrounded by water, it is called an island. When two areas of land are joined by a thin strip of land, the strip is called an isthmus (IS-mus).

**5.** Just as there are landforms, there are also waterforms. Small flows of running water are called streams, branches, or tributaries. All tributaries empty into larger flows of water called rivers. Rivers begin in mountain or hill areas and run downhill. Rivers empty into lakes, oceans, or larger rivers. Where they empty is called the river mouth. Ports and some large cities can be found at the mouths of large rivers.

**6.** An ocean is the largest body of water and is found between continents, which are the largest areas of land. Ocean water that is nearly surrounded by land is known as a gulf. A waterform that is usually smaller than a gulf, more curved, and not as completely surrounded by land as a gulf is called a bay. A sea is a large body of salty water that is mostly or totally surrounded by land.

**7.** Landforms are very important to people. There is a relationship between landforms and the places people settle. Landforms affect where and how people live. If you study a topographic map you will find that large numbers of people tend to live on one type of landform, plains. This is because it is easy to build and farm on plains. Where a large river meets the ocean, or on a plain with good farmland, is often where you will find a large city. Where there is little water, which makes farming hard, and where it is too dry or too cold, there will usually be very few people or cities. You don't find very many big cities on mountains. There are few roads through mountain passes. This is because it is difficult to live and work in the high mountains.

**8.** People learn to live with, or adapt to, their environment. The ways that people dress, how they move goods around, and the crops they plant are the result of their environment. The Inuit dress for and live in a cold environment. Arabs wear long robes to live in desert sand on both hot days and cold nights.

*The California coastline is both rocky and flat. Why is this so?*

*On the Nizhnyaya Tunguska River in the Soviet Union, boats travel in summer and deer sleighs and snowmobiles, in winter. In what other ways do the Soviets adapt to their environment?*

# Building Your Vocabulary

Complete each of the following sentences. Then find and circle each word in the puzzle. The hidden words may be spelled from top to bottom, bottom to top, left to right, right to left, and diagonally. Circle the words as you find them.

```
B A S E M D F K J L M Q S O K I G E C
P L N T O P O G R A P H Y P R T U W T
T L V Y A C F I G N L J H D P B Z X A
M O A S W Y T U R D P K E A L Q N P B
S V B T A R D G I F H E D C A Z X M L
K F J M E O M P Q O O A P N I L K A E
A Q S S U A Y Z B R C A X V N T R W L
E W E D F I U J H M G E P A S S A S A
P D K Q U H I L L S T X Z A V S R M N
L P W Y C G I D S N I A T N U O M O D
W A T E R F A L L E J P M K H F B N Q
X T B K E N V I R O N M E N T C U A Z
```

1. Types of features found on the earth's surface are called _____.

2. The study of landforms on the earth's surface is _____.

3. The conditions in which people live are known as their _____.

4. To become used to something means to _____.

5. High, flat land that rises above the ground around it is a _____.

6. People mostly live and farm on _____.

7. The landforms found between mountains and plains are _____.

8. The highest landforms are _____.

9. The tallest places in a mountain range are _____.

10. The easiest place to get through a mountain is a _____.

11. A river falling over rocks is a _____.

12. A muddy plain is a _____.

13. The driest area on a plain is a _____.

14. Another name for a plateau is a _____.

15. A plateau with very steep sides and a flat top is a _____.

## Using a Topographic Map

Here is a topographic map of North America. Use the map to answer the questions below.

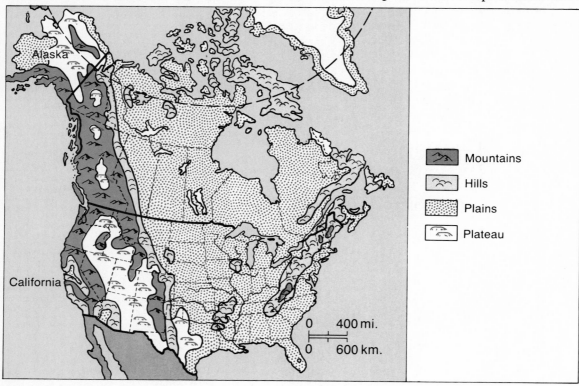

1. Are there mountains near both the East Coast and the West Coast of the United States?

_____

2. Where do you think most farming in the United States is done? Why?

_____

3. Can you see why most people stayed along the East Coast of the United States when it was first being settled? Why didn't the early settlers move deep inland?

_____

4. Why doesn't Alaska have a large population? Name the reasons you can see on the map.

_____

5. Canada grows a lot of wheat. Where would you think most Canadian farmland would be?

_____

6. Why do most people in California live along the coast?

_____

_____

## Identifying Landforms and Waterforms

Locate and label these landforms and waterforms on the diagram at the top of page 35.

| | | | | |
|---|---|---|---|---|
| peninsula | gulf | river mouth | mesa | foothills |
| plains | river | bay | coast | ocean |
| mountains | peak | canyon | plateau | |
| hills | pass | isthmus | island | |

# GEOGRAPHY HIGHLIGHTS

## Tectonic Plates

■ The crust is what makes up the surface of the earth. The earth's crust is divided into plates. The belief that the surface of the earth is built on these plates is called Tectonic Plate theory. As the map shows, there are six main plates and many smaller ones. These plates float on the melted rock which is the center of the earth. As the plates float they rub against each other, slide past each other, or move away from each other. These movements sometimes cause earthquakes, or form mountains and volcanoes. The area where the plates rub the most is found around the Pacific Ocean, called the Pacific Basin. This ring around the Pacific is called the Ring of Fire because so many earthquakes and volcanoes are found there.

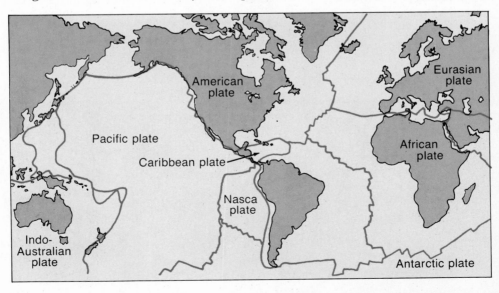

# Chapter 7

## How Does the Spinning Earth Affect Us?

### Reading for a Purpose

1. In which direction does the earth spin?
2. What effect do landforms and water currents have on each other?
3. How does the Coriolis force affect the earth's currents?

### Knowing New Words

**affect** (uh-FEKT)  To influence something.
>  The spinning of the earth **affects** us.

**Coriolis force** (kor-ee-OH-lis FOHRS)  The effect the spinning of the earth has on water and wind currents.
>  The **Coriolis force** makes water currents in the Southern Hemisphere spin differently from water currents in the Northern Hemisphere.

**current** (KUR-unt)  Moving like a river of either air or water.
>  The strong ocean **current** makes swimming dangerous.

**monsoon** (mon-SOON)  Seasonal land and ocean winds.
>  The **monsoon** brought heavy rains this year.

———————— ● ————————

The earth is spinning all the time as it moves through space. The earth's spinning makes the water in the oceans and the air we breathe move. The movements of the larger air and water **currents** can be mapped. At certain times of the year winds can cause a great deal of rain. The winds that cause this rain are called **monsoons**.

### Writing and Thinking

Study the cartoon carefully. Then answer the questions that follow.

36

Use the cartoon on page 36 to answer the questions.

**1.** Why is she throwing the bottle into the ocean?

_____

**2.** Why do bottles travel long distances in the ocean?

_____

_____

**3.** How do you think her father's thoughts explain the way the bottle is moved?

_____

_____

● After reading this chapter, come back to the answers you have written. Make any changes that you think will make your answers better.

# Geography Skills and Concepts

**1.** We live on a spinning earth. As the earth turns, the side pointed toward the sun has daylight. The side of the earth pointed away from the sun has nighttime. It takes 24 hours for the earth to spin around once, which is why there are 24 hours in one day. One complete spin of the earth is called a *rotation*.

**2.** The earth is tilted as it faces the sun. The earth is warmer at the equator and cooler at the poles because of the angle at which the sun's rays meet the earth's surface. There is almost a "direct hit" at the equator.

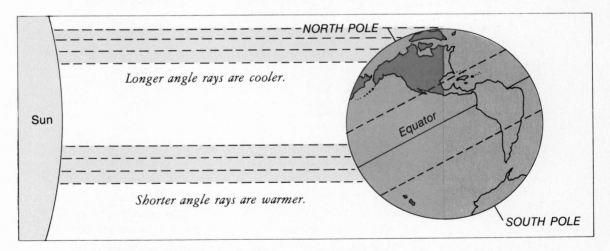

**3.** A large part of the earth is covered with water. As the waters of the oceans move, they strike land. This causes them to move around the land and along the shorelines of the continents. Moving through the ocean waters are **currents**. Currents are like rivers in the ocean. Ocean currents can be mapped. The map on page 38 shows the paths the currents take through the oceans.

**4.** The spinning of the earth **affects** the waters of the ocean. To understand why this is so, fill a jar with water. When the water is still, carefully start to spin the jar. The water will also start to move. The earth's spinning affects the oceans' waters just as the water in your spinning jar was affected.

5. Have you ever noticed that a sink full of water spins as it goes down the drain? It looks like a small whirlpool. You may have heard that a sink full of water spins in the opposite direction when it is emptied in South America. Believe it or not, that is true! This is caused by the spinning of the earth. To understand this, curl the fingers on your right hand to represent the earth. Point your thumb (the North Pole) toward you so you are looking at the way your fingers curl. This is the direction in which the earth spins. Now turn your hand over so that your thumb (the North Pole) is pointed away from you and you are looking at the South Pole. Your fingers look as if they are curled in the other direction, yet you did not change them. The way your fingers are curled shows the direction in which water moves on earth as a result of the way the earth spins. The globe does the same thing when you spin it. Look at the way it spins from the North Pole and then from the South Pole. The earth appears to be spinning in the opposite direction. This spinning makes the water in the Southern Hemisphere move in the opposite direction from the way it moves in the Northern Hemisphere. This effect of the spinning earth on the oceans is called the **Coriolis force**.

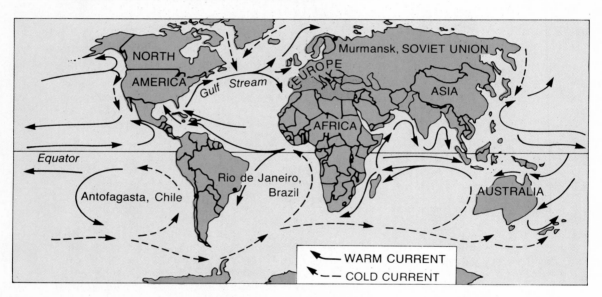

6. This map of the oceans' currents shows how the Coriolis force and the different temperatures of the equator and the poles affect the oceans' currents. Ocean currents have different temperatures. You know that the weather at both poles is cold and the weather near the equator is warm. It makes sense, then, that the water temperature near these places would be the same. However, currents moving through the oceans change the temperature. The waters that are running along the equator are warm. The waters coming from the polar regions are cold. The currents carry the warm waters from the equator to the cooler areas and the cold waters from the poles to the warm areas. That means that cold water from the pole washes along the coast of California while warm water from the equator washes the coast of North Carolina.

7. Does it matter whether ocean water is warm or cold? Yes. Water temperature affects the animal life in the oceans. Warm water is better for most animal life in the oceans. There are some animals that do better in cold water. Shrimp, for example, prefer warm waters, so they are found in the Gulf of Mexico. Lobsters like colder water; they are found off the coast of Maine.

8. The air that surrounds the earth is also affected by the spinning of the earth. The Coriolis force affects winds just as it does water. Wind belts that move one way in the Northern Hemisphere move the other way in the Southern Hemisphere. The winds are also affected by the season of the year. Some winds blow one way during the summer and the other way during the winter. These are called seasonal winds.

9. In many parts of the world there is a wind that blows during certain parts of the year. It is called a **monsoon**, which means "season" in the Arabic language. When the wind comes from the land, the air is dry and there is no rainfall. When the wind comes from warm waters along the equator, it brings heavy monsoon rains. Farmers count on these regular, heavy rains to help their crops. For example, in Bombay, India, there is almost no rainfall from November to March. When the monsoons bring the rain, from June until September there is an average of 88 inches of rainfall! A late monsoon rain or too little rain can ruin farmers' crops.

## Understanding What You Have Read

Choose the words that best complete each statement. Write the letter of your answer in the blank next to the number.

_____ 1. The earth's ocean currents are affected by
a. the equator   b. the spinning of the earth   c. monsoons

_____ 2. Water moving like a river through the oceans is called a
a. current   b. monsoon   c. spin

_____ 3. Wind that causes regular, heavy rains in many parts of the world is called
a. current   b. Bombay   c. a monsoon

_____ 4. Think about how the earth spins. The sun first comes up
a. on the West Coast   b. on the East Coast   c. in the Northern Hemisphere

_____ 5. Water currents in the oceans follow the coastlines because of
a. the Coriolis force   b. landforms   c. the spinning of the earth

## Thinking with Geography

Study the map of the oceans' currents on page 38 to answer these questions.

1. The Soviet Union has a terrible problem with freezing ports during the long winters. Why doesn't the port of Murmansk freeze? Why do you think that Murmansk is so important to the Soviet Union?

_____

_____

2. Why is the water off the coast of Maine cold enough for lobsters while the water off the coast of North Carolina is warm enough for shrimp?

_____

3. Look at Antofagasta, Chile, and Rio de Janeiro, Brazil. They are at almost the same latitude, yet Rio de Janeiro gets about 60 inches of rain per year. Antofagasta gets only about 10 inches of rain per year. How can you explain this difference?

_____

_____

## The Seasons

■  We live on a tilting world. The earth is always tilted. It takes the earth one year to circle the sun once. As the earth revolves around the sun, the sun's rays strike the earth at different angles. The angle of the sun's rays causes the seasons. The more tilted the sun's rays are when they strike the earth, the cooler they are. The more direct the rays are, the warmer they are. Look at the diagram. When the North Pole is tilted away from the sun, its rays do not reach higher than 66½°N latitude. That is the Arctic Circle. When the South Pole is tilted toward the sun, it strikes most directly at 23½°S, which is the Tropic of Capricorn. When this happens, the Northern Hemispere has winter, and the Southern Hemisphere has summer. When the North Pole is tilted toward the sun, the sun strikes most directly at 23½°N, which is the Tropic of Cancer. When the South Pole is tilted away from the sun, its rays do not reach higher than 66½°S latitude. That is the Antarctic Circle. During this time, the Northern Hemisphere has summer and the Southern Hemisphere has winter. Spring and fall occur when the North and South Poles are at a 90° angle from the sun.

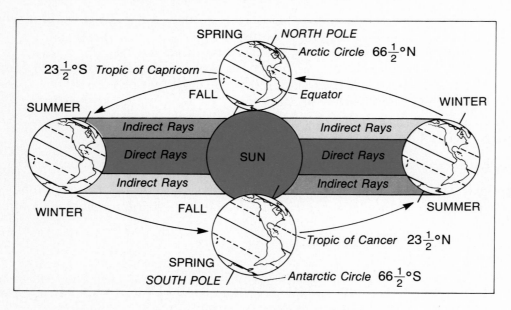

# Chapter 8

## How Are Rivers and Rainfall Related?

**Reading for a Purpose**

1. Where does rainfall come from?
2. How are rainfall and rivers related?
3. How are rivers made?

## Knowing New Words

condensation (kon-den-SAY-shun)   To cool down and change from vapor to water.
   The glass in the warm room had **condensation** on it.

evaporation (ih-vap-uh-RAY-shun)   To warm up and change from water to vapor.
   In the noon heat the water in the dog's dish disappeared through **evaporation**.

vapor (VAY-pur)   The steam that is made by heating a liquid.
   As the sun set, we could see **vapor** rising from the lake.

⎯⎯⎯⎯⎯◼ ● ◻⎯⎯⎯⎯⎯

Rainfall comes from water **vapor** in the air. As the vapor cools, the water is released as rainfall. When a lot of rain falls in one area, it runs off into streams. The runoff collects into rivers, which empty into oceans or lakes.

## Writing and Thinking

Study the cartoon carefully. Then answer the questions that follow.

1. Do you think that rainfall and geography are related? Explain your answer.

_____

_____

_____

2. Where do you think that rainfall comes from?

_____

3. Where do you think that rivers come from?

_____

4. What do you think the mother's answer was? Write her answer in the cartoon bubble.

● After you have read this chapter, come back to the answers you have written. Make any changes that you think will make your answers better.

41

# Geography Skills and Concepts

1.  Where does the water that falls as rain come from? New water is not made every time it rains. Rain is part of a continuing cycle, or circle, of water falling to the earth and returning to the sky. How does this cycle work?

2.  To answer that question, fill a shallow bowl with water and put it on a windowsill in strong sunlight. As the water gets warmer, it will disappear by turning into water vapor. This is called **evaporation**. Now there is water vapor in the air. To see the vapor, fill a glass with ice and water. Soon the outside of the glass will fog up and start to drip the water. Did the glass leak? No. When the water vapor in the warm air hit the cold glass, the water vapor cooled and turned to water. This is called **condensation**.

3.  Rainfall is made in the same way. Water, from the ocean or other bodies of water, evaporates into the air. The warmer the air, the more water vapor it can hold. Air that is cool or cold cannot hold water vapor the way warmer air can. The water vapor condenses, or turns to liquid, as rainfall.

4.  Winds carry moist air from over the ocean onto land. When the air meets landforms such as mountains, the wind is forced upward and the air cools. When the air cools, the water vapor condenses into rainfall. This happens on the windward side of the mountain. The side of the mountain that faces away from the wind is the dry side. As the air moves down the mountain, it warms, and rain does not occur. This is the leeward side of the mountain. This is shown in the diagram below.

5.  Rivers are formed when there is regular rainfall over a wide area. The rain washes down the sides of mountains and forms small creeks. The creeks run together as streams, and the streams run together to make a river. Finally, the rivers either run into lakes or into the oceans, and the cycle starts all over again. Evaporation prevents the oceans from filling and covering the earth.

6.  Why are some rivers larger than others? There are three things that affect the size of a river: (a) the amount of condensation and rainfall over the area where the river gets its water; (b) other rivers flowing, or emptying, into it; and (c) the size of the area where the rainfall empties into the river. The area where the rainfall drains into the river is called the *watershed*. The larger watershed area and the more rain that falls into it, the bigger the river will be.

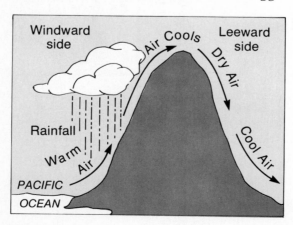

**7.** Which river do you think is the greatest river in North America? Here is a chart that shows the greatest rivers in North America. The chart shows the length of each river, its watershed area, and the volume or amount of water it carries.

| River | Length (miles long) | Watershed Area (square miles) | Volume of Water (cubic feet per second) |
|---|---|---|---|
| Mississippi | 2,350 | 1,220 | 610,000 |
| Mackenzie | 2,514 | 700 | 280,000 |
| St. Lawrence | 1,945 | 460 | 500,000 |
| Nelson | 1,600 | 440 | 80,000 |
| Yukon | 1,979 | 320 | 180,000 |

Rivers can be called great based on the distance they travel, their use to humans, or the amount of water they carry. The Mississippi River is not as long as the Mackenzie River in Canada, but it has a larger watershed area. It carries more than twice the amount of water that the Mackenzie carries.

**8.** Probably the greatest river in the world is the Amazon River in Brazil. It is 3,900 miles long, far longer than the Mississippi River in the United States. The Amazon River is not as long as the Nile River in Northern Africa, which is 4,160 miles long. But the Amazon has a watershed area that is nearly as large as the continental United States—over two million square miles! It moves, at the sea where it empties, over 7,600,000 cubic feet of water per second. That is more than the Mississippi, the Nile, and China's mighty Yangtze (YANG-see) rivers put together! It would take 21 Mississippi rivers to move that much water!

**9.** What makes the Amazon River so large? The wind carries the moist air over the warm ocean onto the land and toward huge mountains, creating a great amount of rain. All of the rainfall empties into one huge watershed to form the Amazon. Six large rivers also empty into the Amazon. Nowhere else in the world do so many forces affecting the size of a river come together as they do in the Amazon.

*The Nile River (left). The Amazon River (right). How are these two rivers similar and different?*

## Understanding What You Have Read

Fill in the blanks with the missing words. Choose your words from the list below.

evaporate          empty          warm

cooled          condenses          area

watershed          water          condensation

Rainfall comes from _____ vapor in the air. That comes from
(1)

_____ water that is heated by the sun. Cold water does not
(2)

_____ as quickly. When the water _____ into rain-
(3)                                              (4)

fall, it has been _____ off. Cold air does not hold as much water as
(5)

warm air.

Rainfall that drains into a large area called a _____ empties into
(6)

streams and rivers. Three things affect the size of rivers: (a) the amount of

_____ and rainfall over the area; (b) other rivers that
(7)

_____ into the river; and (c) the size of the _____
(8)                                                                          (9)

where the rainfall empties into the river.

# GEOGRAPHY HIGHLIGHTS

## The Powerful Colorado River

■ Which is better at moving dirt, a river or a bulldozer? As you stand at the rim of the Grand Canyon in Arizona and look down, you will see a narrow river, the Colorado. Could that little river be better than a bulldozer at moving dirt?

As a river works its way through an area, it erodes (ih-ROHDS), or tears dirt away from, the banks on either side of the river and carries the dirt downstream. By erosion, the Colorado River dug a canyon 280 miles long, which is over 1 mile deep! No wonder the river looks small from the rim! The middle of the canyon the river has dug is over 9 miles wide!

Each day the Colorado carries off 391,780 tons of dirt. That is enough to fill 80,000 dump trucks with 5 tons of dirt each! If that many dump trucks were to work every day, one would have to be filled almost every second during a 24-hour day to carry off that much dirt! Do you think a bulldozer is as powerful as the mighty Colorado?

# Unit 2 Review

## Building Your Vocabulary

Complete the crossword puzzle.

**Across**

2. One-half of the earth.
5. The steam that is made by heating a liquid.
6. The features or landforms on the surface of the earth.
7. Moving like a river of either air or water.
8. High, flat land that rises above the ground around it.
12. To change the shape of something.
13. One of the seven largest land masses of the earth.
14. To become used to something.

**Down**

1. Seasonal land and sea winds.
3. Warming up and changing from water to vapor.
4. The conditions in which people live.
7. Cooling down and changing from vapor to water.
9. Types of features found on the earth's land areas.
10. The force that comes from the spinning of the earth.
11. To influence something.

## Understanding What You Have Read

Fill in the blanks with the words that best complete each sentence. Choose the best word for each blank from the word bank below. The completed sentences can be used as a review of Unit 2.

rainfall          plane          gulf
mountains         four           waterforms
cartographer      project        peninsula
plains            cylinder       distortion
Coriolis force    spinning       landforms
equator           topographic    bay
cone              plateaus       hills
east              condenses

A person who draws maps is a _____. There is no way to make
a round surface flat without changing it. To draw a map, a decision about what
_____ to use must be made. There are basically three different ways
to _____, or show, the world as a map. It can be done as a
_____, a _____, and a _____.
When a cartographer draws land features, they can be classified as
_____ types of _____. There are (a)
_____, which are often used for farming, (b)
_____, which are rolling land rising from the land around them, (c)
_____, which are high, hilly land, and (d) _____,
which are high, flat lands, rising from the ground around them. A
_____ map tells the reader what landforms there are in a mapped
area. A narrow strip of land surrounded by water on three sides is called a
_____.

Water types can be mapped as _____. A waterform that is usually
smaller than a _____ is called a _____.

We live on a _____ earth. The force that makes things in the
Southern Hemisphere move away from things in the Northern Hemisphere is called the
_____. The earth spins toward the _____. The
earth's ocean currents are warmest at the _____, where the air holds a
lot of water due to its warmth. As the air cools, the water in it _____
into _____.

46

## Identifying Places

This is a map of the imaginary country of Austrogalia. Locate and label the 11 topographic features on the map. Then answer the questions that follow.

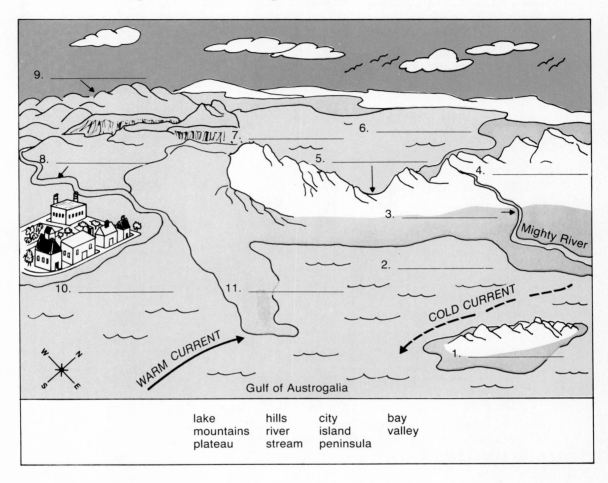

lake        hills      city        bay
mountains   river      island      valley
plateau     stream     peninsula

1. Where does the Mighty River begin? How was it formed? Explain.

_____

_____

2. What do you think the topography between the area of the bay and the Gulf of Austrogalia is like? Explain your answer.

_____

_____

3. What part of the island do you think gets the most rainfall? Explain your answer.

_____

_____

_____

# Chapter 9

## Climate and People's Lives

### Reading for a Purpose

1. What is climate?
2. How are climates different?
3. How does climate affect people's lives?
4. How does climate affect trade between nations?

### Knowing New Words

**precipitation** (prih-sip-ih-TAY-shun)   Moisture that falls to earth in the form of hail, mist, rain, sleet, or snow.
The **precipitation** in my area is usually in the form of rain.

**frost** (FROST)   Ice crystals that are formed when water vapor freezes.
**Frost** covered the ground like a thin blanket on a cold morning.

———— • ————

The part of geography that affects people's lives the most is **climate**. People's choice of food, homes, and clothing is affected by climate. Climate strongly affects what items nations trade with each other. This chapter will help you to find out about these and other ways that climate affects your life.

### Writing and Thinking

Study the cartoon carefully. Then answer the questions that follow.

MOVING TO A NEW PLACE. WHAT IS THE CLIMATE LIKE?

Use the cartoon on page 48 to answer the questions.

1. What do you think the man, the woman, and the farmer are saying? Fill in the missing words in the cartoon balloons.

2. Explain at least three ways that climate will affect these people's lives.

_____

_____

_____

● After reading this chapter, come back to the answers you have written. Make any changes that you think will make your answers better.

# Geography Skills and Concepts

1. Climate and weather do not mean the same thing. The weather report usually tells you how hot or cold, wet or dry it will be on a given day. Some reports tell about a few days at a time. The report tells you if you can expect rain or snow. This is weather. Climate, however, means the kind of weather a place has over a long period of time—what it is like year after year.

2. To find out about climate, you must ask three questions. How hot or cold is it over a long period of time? How much rain falls throughout the year? How long is the growing season? Can you answer these questions about where you live? If you can, you have a good idea of your area's climate.

3. Is your area hot or cold? *Temperature* is the amount of heat or cold in the air. Temperature can change quickly. It can be very hot in the daytime and cold at night. However, as a student of geography you must be more interested in temperature changes throughout a season than in daily changes. For example, the average daily temperature of New York City during the winter is 34 degrees Fahrenheit. The average temperature during the summer is 76 degrees Fahrenheit. This should tell you that New York City has warm summers and cold winters. In San Francisco, the average winter temperature is 52 degrees Fahrenheit. In the summer the average temperature is 63 degrees Fahrenheit. This should tell you that San Francisco is neither too hot nor too cold the year round.

4. Is your area wet or dry? There are many kinds of moisture that fall on earth. Rain, snow, sleet, and hail are all forms of **precipitation**. To understand the climate in an area you must know about its precipitation. Some places have rain or snow all year round. Other places have rain only at certain times of the year. Some places have little or no rain at all.

5. The average rainfall in an area is measured over a long period of time. Rainfall is measured by the number of inches of rain that falls within a given time. It is possible to measure rainfall during a season or during a year. For example, the average rainfall for six summer months in Charleston, South Carolina, is 30 inches. During the winter, the average is only 15 inches. This should tell you that the summer months receive a lot of rain and that the winter months are fairly dry.

**6.** Is the growing season in your area long or short? Another part of climate is the length of the growing season. This is the length of time that a place is free from **frost**, that is, free from freezing temperatures. This is very important for farmers. Farmers can plant only those crops that can be grown during the area's growing season. The growing season is the time after the last frost in the spring and before the first frost in the fall. Usually, the farther away a place is from the equator, the shorter the growing season.

**7.** Climate affects the kind of clothing and homes that people have. The desert people of the Middle East wear loose-fitting cotton clothing. This helps to keep them cool in the hot desert. In the highlands of the Middle East people wear clothing made of wool or leather to keep warm. The Inuit in northern Canada may live in a house of snow, whereas people who live in dry areas, of course, could not. These people might live in homes made of sun-dried brick or mud.

**8.** Differences in climate mean differences in temperature, precipitation, and the length of the growing season. This helps to explain the differences in how people live and work. It also helps to explain why some nations trade with each other. Some parts of the world have a lot of rain, whereas other parts are dry. Thus, farmers cannot grow the same crops throughout the world. Wheat can be grown in many kinds of climates, but olives and some other crops need a dry climate. We know which crops grow best in our climate. Hawaii's climate is perfect for growing sugarcane and pineapples. The midwestern part of the United States is good for growing corn and wheat. Farmers in the United States cannot grow all of the crops the people may want to eat or use for different products. People in other nations face the same problem. So different nations trade with one another to get the products they need.

## Understanding What You Have Read

Choose the words that best complete each statement. Write the letter of your answer in the blank next to the number.

_____ 1. The main idea of paragraphs 1–6 is to describe the
a. meaning of temperature   b. meaning of precipitation
c. meaning of climate

_____ 2. The growing season refers to the
a. time between the last and first frost   b. amount of rainfall in a place
c. climate of a place

_____ 3. Growing seasons become shorter as you travel
a. toward the equator   b. away from the equator
c. toward the South Pole

_____ 4. When the weather forecaster says that "tomorrow will be cloudy," you are being told about
a. weather   b. climate   c. rainfall

_____ 5. Climate will make a difference in the amount of
a. minerals a nation has   b. steel a nation can make   c. water farmers can use

_____ 6. Climate will make a difference in the farm products a nation will trade
a. for   b. away   c. both of these

_____ 7. Climate will affect the kinds of clothing people wear, the crops they grow, and the
a. type of houses they live in   b. television programs they enjoy seeing
c. newspapers they enjoy reading

# Chapter 10

## What Are the Reasons for Differences in Climate?

**Reading for a Purpose**

What are five reasons for differences in climate?

### Knowing New Words

influence (IN-floo-uns)   A force that can affect something or someone's actions.
   The teacher **influenced** me to do my homework.

altitude (AL-tih-tood)   The height of land above sea level.
   Temperatures become lower as the **altitude** gets higher.

Within the United States there are differences in climate. Throughout the world there is an even greater variety of climates. Why is this so? This chapter explains five reasons for differences in climate.

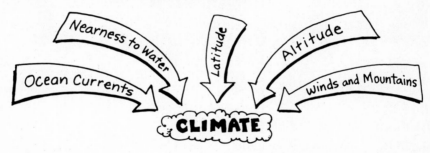

### Writing and Thinking

Answer the following questions about climate.

1. How do you think ocean currents affect climates?

2. How do you think latitude, or distance from the equator, **influences** climate?

3. How do you think nearness to water affects climate?

4. How do you think **altitude,** or distance above sea level, determines climate?

5. How do you think winds and mountains determine climate?

● After reading this chapter, come back to the answers you have written. Make any changes or corrections that you think will make your answers better.

# Geography Skills and Concepts

**1.** The most important influence on climate is latitude, or the distance from the equator. If two places in the world are located the same distance from water, at the same altitude, and the same distance from the equator, they will have the same climate. Look at Map 1. Notice that those places that are farther from the equator have colder temperatures. Notice also that it does not matter whether the place is north or south of the equator. The closer you go to the equator, the warmer the temperature becomes. This is because at the equator the sun's rays are direct. Thus they are stronger and hotter. As you travel away from the equator, to the north or south, the sun's rays slant and become weaker. Therefore, it becomes cooler.

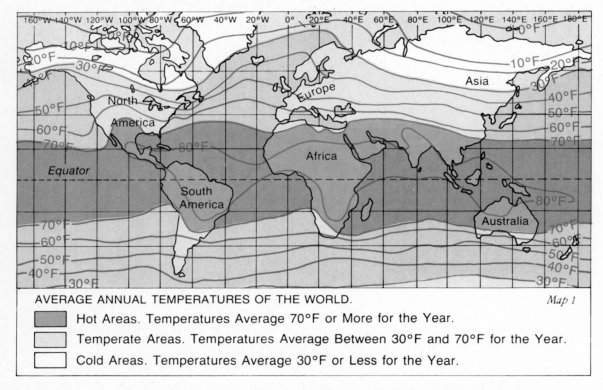

AVERAGE ANNUAL TEMPERATURES OF THE WORLD.    *Map 1*

▓ Hot Areas. Temperatures Average 70°F or More for the Year.

░ Temperate Areas. Temperatures Average Between 30°F and 70°F for the Year.

□ Cold Areas. Temperatures Average 30°F or Less for the Year.

**2.** Altitude, the elevation or height of land above sea level, also affects climate. Air grows cooler as you travel upward, away from the surface of the earth. Look at Diagram 1 on page 53. The diagram shows two cities in South America. They are Quito, the capital of Ecuador, and Manaus, a city in Brazil. Notice that both cities are very close to the equator. However, there is a big difference in temperature between the two cities. Why? Part of the reason is that Quito is located in the highlands of the Andes Mountains and Manaus is located in the lowlands. The altitude affects the temperature of the cities. Thus Quito has a pleasant climate, whereas Manaus is hot and wet.

**3.** Winds and mountains also determine climate. If the winds blow in from the warm ocean, they will carry moisture with them. Rain will fall when the air cools. If the winds blow from the land out to sea, they will be dry winds, because they do not have as much moisture. Look at Diagram 2 on page 53. It shows what happens in the western part of the United States. The winds from the Pacific Ocean carry moisture with them. As the winds meet the mountains

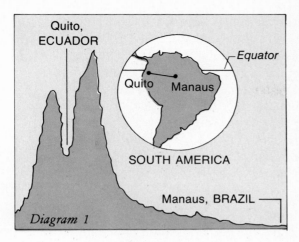

Diagram 1

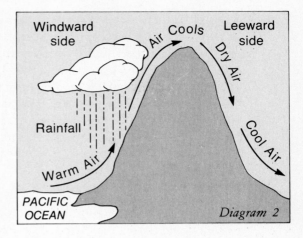

Diagram 2

along the West Coast, the air rises and is cooled. When the air cools, the clouds can no longer hold the moisture. Therefore, it rains on the western side of the mountains. Here you will find thick, green forests and lots of plants. After the air has crossed the mountains, it is drier. Thus the land east of the mountains receives little rainfall and, in many places, deserts are formed. This occurs in many other places in the world.

**4.** Not all the winds of the earth blow continually from the same direction. There are shifting, or changing, local winds. These winds are caused by the heating or cooling of land. The monsoons of Asia are an example of this. When the winds blow from the land, they are dry and cold. However, when the winds blow from the Indian Ocean, they are warm and wet, bringing humid weather and heavy rains. Do you think you can draw two diagrams that would help to explain monsoons? Try it.

**5.** Ocean currents affect climate in many parts of the world. As you learned earlier, currents are like fast-flowing streams of water within a larger body of water. Currents can carry either warm or cool water from one part of the world to another. Winds are affected by the temperatures of the ocean currents. Look at Map 2 below. Notice that these currents travel great distances. Look again

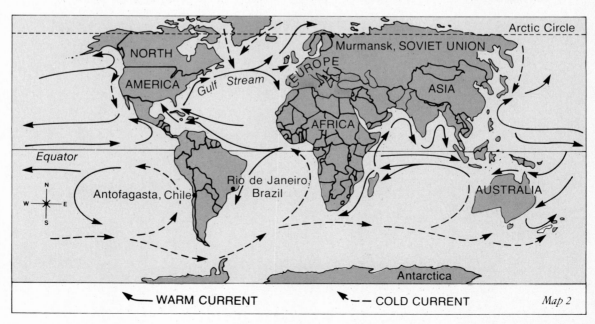

Map 2

53

at Maps 1 and 2. Look at the area in northwest Europe. Notice that the land is in the Arctic Circle, yet the temperatures are above freezing. This is because the land is warmed by an ocean current called the Gulf Stream. The Gulf Stream is a warm ocean current that begins in the warm waters of the Gulf of Mexico. It flows northward along the eastern coast of the United States toward Newfoundland. Then it turns eastward and crosses the Atlantic Ocean. The winds blowing above the ocean current are warm winds. These warm winds blow across England and much of northwestern Europe. As a result, the people of those lands enjoy a warmer climate than others living at the same latitudes. By comparing Map 1 and Map 2, you can find other lands that are either warmed or cooled by ocean currents.

**6.** Nearness to water also affects climate. Water is slower to heat up or to cool down than air is. Places that are near large bodies of water have a more "even" temperature than places in the same latitude that are not near water. This helps to explain what is shown in Map 3 below. It compares the average winter temperatures in New York City, New York, and Omaha, Nebraska. Both cities have almost the same latitude. However, there is a big difference in their temperatures throughout the year. Omaha is not near a large body of water. Therefore, temperatures in Omaha reach 100 degrees Fahrenheit in summer and may drop to 10 degrees Fahrenheit below zero in winter. The average winter temperatures in Omaha are 23 degrees Fahrenheit in winter and 79 degrees Fahrenheit in summer. New York City is on the Atlantic Ocean. Because of the nearness to water, the temperature there hardly ever reaches 100 degrees Fahrenheit in summer or zero in winter. The average temperatures in New York City are 33 degrees Fahrenheit in winter and 77 degrees Fahrenheit in summer. Omaha may have a difference of 110 degrees Fahrenheit in temperature during a year. New York is likely to have only a difference of 80 degrees throughout the year. Nearness to or distance from a large body of water is what makes the difference.

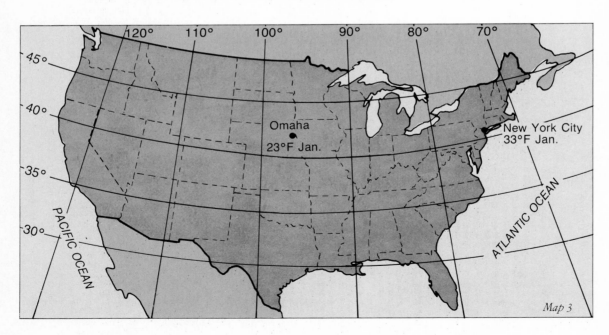

*Map 3*

## Understanding What You Have Read

Write *true* next to each statement that is true. If the statement is false, write *false* in the space provided and change the underlined word or words to make the statement true.

_____ 1. When wet winds blow toward mountains, the side that gets the most rain is the side from which the wind came.

_____ 2. Some large cities that are on the equator, such as Quito, Ecuador, attract people because of their high latitude.

_____ 3. The western side of the mountains along the Pacific Coast receives more rain than the eastern side because the Gulf Stream brings warm winds.

_____ 4. In general, the farther a land is from the equator, the warmer its climate.

_____ 5. As you climb higher above sea level, temperatures become cooler.

_____ 6. As you move farther from large bodies of water, there is a smaller difference in temperature throughout the year.

_____ 7. Rainfall is greatest where land borders a cold part of the ocean.

_____ 8. Winds that blow from the land are dry winds.

_____ 9. Many deserts are formed because ocean currents block the rain.

_____ 10. Climates are the same throughout the world.

## Making a Map

In the space provided draw a map of an imaginary land. Show how your imaginary land is affected by at least three of the five things that affect climate. Include all of the following:

1. A legend or key
2. A scale of miles
3. A title
4. The latitude lines to show how far the land is from the equator
5. Any topographic features such as mountains, lakes, oceans, and so on

Explain which things on your map affect the climate of your imaginary land.

_____

_____

# Chapter 11

# Different Kinds of Climate

**Reading for a Purpose**

1. What are the different kinds of climate regions?
2. What is each climate region like?
3. What is meant by low, middle, and high latitudes?
4. Where are some of the climate regions found?

## Knowing New Words

**climate region** (KLY-mit REE-jun)   A space on earth that has a particular climate.
The tropical rain-forest **climate region** is found in some places on or near the equator.

———————●———————

There are many kinds of **climate regions** in the world. In this chapter the climate regions are divided by the latitudes at which they usually appear. This will help you to locate them. Low-latitude areas are between 0 and $23\frac{1}{2}$ degrees, both north and south of the equator. These places are closest to the equator. Middle-latitude areas are between $23\frac{1}{2}$ and $66\frac{1}{2}$ degrees, both north and south of the equator. These places are between the low latitudes and the North and South poles. High-latitude areas are between $66\frac{1}{2}$ degrees and the poles. The diagram below shows the low, middle, and high latitudes.

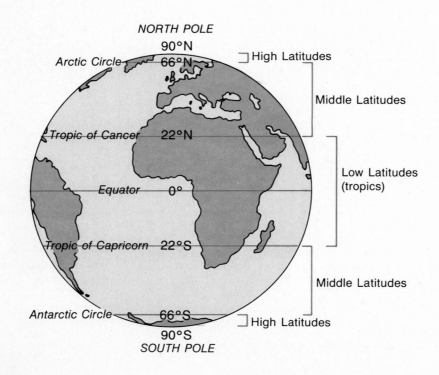

# Writing and Thinking

Use the pictures of the three climate zones to help you complete the chart below.

| Climate Zone | Latitude (Low, Middle, High) | Temperature | Amount of Rainfall | Looks Like |
|---|---|---|---|---|
| Rain Forest | | | | |
| Savanna | | | | |
| Desert | | | | |

● After reading this chapter, come back to the answers you have written. Make any changes that you think will make your answers better.

### Low-Latitude Climates

**1.** *Tropical rain forests* have the hot, wet climate found in the low lands near the equator. Large rain forests are located in parts of South America, central Africa, and Southeast Asia. Trees in rain forests usually grow to over 100 feet tall. The trees are of great variety, including rubber, bamboo, teak, and mahogany. In the rain forest the sun shines all year, but because of all the trees, little of the sun reaches the jungle floor. Though it is hot, the temperatures seldom rise above 90 degrees Fahrenheit. Some rain falls in the rain forests almost every day. It is always damp and sticky there. Rivers are the main highways of tropical forests.

**2.** Another low-latitude climate is the *savanna,* or grassland. It is usually found both north and south of the rain forests. Savannas are the "lands of two seasons." There is a winter dry season and a summer wet season. During the dry season there is little or no rain. The grasses turn brown and the water in the streams gets very low. It is very hot and dry. During the rainy season, the rain pours down day after day. The ground then becomes soft and muddy. It is hot and sticky during the rainy season.

**3.** North and south of the grasslands, but still mostly in the low latitudes, are many of the world's *deserts.* Deserts are lands that receive less than 10 inches of rainfall a year. They may be sandy, rocky, hilly, or even cold. What all deserts have in common is that they are very dry. Low-latitude deserts are the driest and hottest parts of the earth. The most famous desert in the low latitudes is the Sahara in Africa. The Sahara is as large in area as the mainland of the United States. Other low-latitude deserts are the Arabian in the Middle East and the deserts that cover most of Australia. In a desert the difference in temperature between day and night is very great. The land cools off quickly when the sun goes down. The temperature may drop as much as 50 degrees. Few people live in the desert. However, desert soils are not all poor. Some desert areas have been known to bloom when they have been properly watered.

### Middle-Latitude Climates

**4.** *Mediterranean* climate areas are pleasant, sunny lands. The growing season in these lands usually lasts all year. Mediterranean climate is noted for its mild, rainy winters and dry summers. This type of climate is found on the western coast of countries between 30 and 40 degrees latitude, north and south of the equator. A Mediterranean climate is found mostly in California, central Chile, South Africa, and around the Mediterranean Sea. This type of climate zone is small but well settled. Many crops are grown in this region, such as fruit, grain, and flowers. Farming is usually difficult because of the dry summers. Most Mediterranean lands are mountainous. These lands are popular among tourists.

**5.** *Humid-subtropical* climate is found in the moist places just north and south of the tropics. These areas are located on the eastern side of their continents. Humid-subtropical climate is found along the southeastern coast of the United States, South America, Australia, Japan, and mainland China. Warm ocean currents flow along these coasts. Thus winds blowing across these currents bring warm, moist air. Most areas with this climate have rainfall throughout the year. These areas also have rich soil. Therefore, a variety of crops can be grown, such as cotton, grains, tobacco, peanuts, rice, vegetables, and fruit. Many of these crops can be grown more than once a year. As you would expect, more people live in this climate region than in any other.

*A rice field in China's Guizhou province. Why do you think most of the farm work is done by hand?*

6. *Marine* climate is one that many people prefer. It is mild and has plenty of rain and a long growing season. The word *marine,* of course, refers to water. All of the lands with this climate are near or are surrounded by water. Differences in temperatures between summer and winter and from year to year are very little. This is because of the warming ocean currents that flow near these lands. Marine climate is found in the Pacific Northwest of the United States, Pacific Canada, Western Europe, the British Isles, southern Chile, and New Zealand. Cities with this climate are San Francisco, California, and London, England.

7. *Humid-continental* climate is the "climate of the four seasons"—autumn, winter, spring, and summer. This climate is more influenced by winds that pass over the land than by winds that pass over the ocean. It is called humid because there is enough rainfall for a variety of crops. Summers are hot, and winters are cold. As you move inland, there is a greater difference in temperature throughout the year. Some of the best farmlands in the world are found in this climate zone. Humid-continental climate is found in the northern and central United States, the central part of the Soviet Union, northern China, and southern Canada. People living in this climate region are used to the changing seasons and the great differences in temperature.

8. *Continental steppe* (STEP) is another middle-latitude climate zone. In the interior of large continents far from the ocean breezes are the dry flatlands. These regions are called prairies, or Great Plains, in the United States and Canada. In Argentina they are called the pampas. In Asia they are called steppes. Summers are hot and winters are cold in these regions, as in humid-continental areas. However, rainfall is light and uncertain in the steppe climate. Ten to twenty inches of rain a year is normal. It rains mostly in spring and summer. Grass grows where there is enough rain. Most of the world's wheat is grown in this climate zone.

9. Continental steppes are right next to *continental deserts.* These places receive less than 10 inches of rainfall a year. The Southwest United States, the Gobi of Asia, and smaller deserts in Peru, Chile, and Africa are all continental deserts. Land in this region cannot be farmed without irrigation because there is so little rainfall. Herding is the most important kind of farm work. However, because there is not much grass, herds and flocks must be moved over a wide area.

### High-Latitude Climates

**10.** Few if any people live in the high latitude climate zones. This is because these regions are extremely cold. There are two kinds of high-latitude climates. They are called tundra and taiga (TY-guh). These are both Russian words. *Tundra* means "marshy plain." This climate is found in the northern areas of Canada, Europe, and the Soviet Union. The winters are very cold. The ground is usually frozen except during the short summer months, when it is mushy. No crops can be raised, and few people live there. In the far north and south is the ice cap region. It is cold all year round. These areas are being studied by many scientists. They have found minerals and learned about the climate, weather, and ocean life in the tundra regions.

**11.** South of the tundra is the *taiga,* a word which means "forest" in Russian. The region contains the largest forests in the world. It is also rich in minerals and fur-bearing animals. Here too the summers are short and the winters very cold and long. Few people live here. Among those who do are lumberers, trappers, fishers, miners, and traders.

**12.** One of the most interesting climates is the *vertical climate*. This climate is formed by high mountains that make a climate of their own. Do you think the side of a mountain could possibly have all the climate zones discussed in this chapter? The higher up a mountain you go, the cooler the temperature. If a very high mountain was located on low lands near the equator, it would have the full range of temperatures. Therefore, it would have tropical climates near its base. As you moved up the mountain, it would get colder with climate zones similar to those mentioned in this chapter.

## Understanding What You Have Read

Use the terms in this list to identify the climate regions described below.

desert climate     tropical rain forest climate     humid-continental climate
taiga and/or tundra climate     continental steppe climate     Mediterranean climate
vertical climate     marine climate     humid-subtropical climate

1. This climate is found in the low lands near the equator. It is hot and very rainy all year long. What climate is it?

2. These climates are found in the high latitudes. They have very short summers and long, cold winters. They are lonely as few people live there. What climates are they?

3. This climate is found in the middle latitudes. It has four seasons. This climate is found on several continents. It has some of the best farmlands in the world. What climate is it?

4. This climate is found along the eastern side of continents in the middle latitudes. It is just north and south of the tropics. It has rainfall all year long. More people live here than in any other climate zone. What climate is it?

5. This climate is a very mountainous climate. On the side of one of its tall mountains you will find many different climate zones. What climate is it?

**6.** This climate is found in the interior of large continents. It is also the middle latitudes. It has lots of flat lands called prairies, or plains. It gets only 10 to 20 inches of rainfall a year. Its name came from Asia. What climate is it?

_____

**7.** This climate has hot, dry summers and mild, rainy winters. Its growing season is all year. It is found on the western coasts of countries in the middle latitudes. What climate is it?

_____

**8.** This climate is found in the middle latitudes. Its temperature is nearly the same all year long. It has lots of rain and a long growing season. Lands with this climate are near or are surrounded by water. What climate is it?

_____

**9.** This climate is found at many different latitudes. It can be hot or cold. It always gets less than 10 inches of rainfall a year. What climate is it?

_____

_____

## Outlining

Complete the missing parts of the following outline.

**Different Kinds of Climate**

1. Low latitudes: Zero degrees to _____ degrees north and south latitude. (Often called tropical climate.)

    **A.** _____   **B.** _____   **C.** Deserts

2. Middle latitudes: _____ degrees to _____ degrees north and south latitude. (Often called temperate climate.)

    **A.** Mediterranean   **B.** Humid-subtropical   **C.** _____

    **D.** _____   **E.** Continental steppe   **F.** _____

3. _____ latitudes: _____ degrees to the poles.

    **A.** _____   **B.** _____   **C.** Vertical

---

# GEOGRAPHY ◆ HIGHLIGHTS

## Deserts

■ What is desertification? Deserts are growing, expanding parts of the world's geography. This growth is called desertification. An example of a growing desert is the southern part of the Sahara. This area is called the Sahel. The area had a long period in which it had no rain, called a drought, that began in 1968. During the next six years the Sahel became a desert. Over 250,000 people died in the growing desert. Desertification is a serious problem. Every year the world's deserts grow.

# Unit 3 Review

## Reading a World Climate Map

Read the statements below. Tell whether you agree or disagree with each statement. Use the world climate map to help you explain your answer.

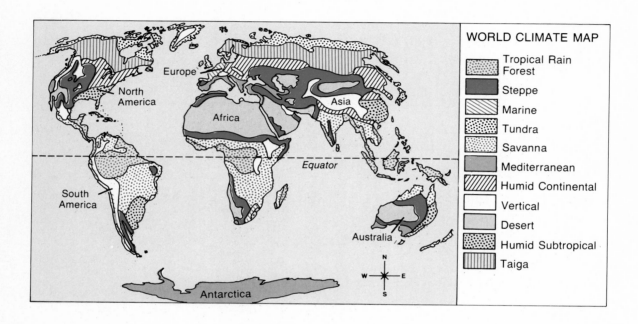

1. North America has most of the world's climates.

   _____

   _____

2. The largest climate area in North America is humid-continental.

   _____

   _____

3. North America has climates people like to live in.

   _____

   _____

4. North America has better climates for growing crops than many parts of Eastern Europe.

   _____

   _____

5. The deserts of the world are found only near the equator.

_____

_____


6. Vertical climates can be found on all continents.

_____

_____


7. A large part of the world has climates that are not suitable for people.

_____

_____


8. It is possible for an area on the equator to have many different kinds of climate.

_____

_____


9. Each area of the world can only grow certain kinds of crops.

_____

_____


10. Low-, middle-, and high-latitude climates are found on both sides of the equator.

_____

_____


11. The continent of Africa has the same climate zones both north and south of the equator.

_____

_____


12. It could be said that different kinds of plants and trees grow throughout the world.

_____

_____


13. It could be said that it is easier for people to live in some parts of the world than in others.

_____

_____


14. The climate zones of the world influence the way people live.

_____

_____

## Making Inferences

Making an inference is making an educated guess from the information that you have. In the space provided write the name of the climate zone or zones that you think best answer each question.

1. Where would the average person probably be unable to live because of the cold?

   _____

2. Where would little or nothing grow unless water were brought in?

   _____

3. Where would you find that rivers instead of roads are often used to transport people and products?

   _____

4. Where would there be very cold winters and very hot summers?

   _____

5. Where could you grow products all year round?

   _____

   _____

## Living Your Geography

Answer each of the following questions by applying your geographic knowledge to your own life. You may refer to the chapters in this unit to help you answer the questions.

1. Locate your hometown or the nearest large city on a map. It is located at _____

   degrees (north/south) latitude and _____ degrees (east/west) longitude.
2. What is the climate like in your area? Describe it.

   _____

3. Which geographical facts, such as distance from the equator, physical features, or distance from a large body of water, have influenced your climate zone?

   _____

   _____

4. Is there any kind of work done in your area that is strongly influenced by the climate?

   _____

   _____

5. Are any of the games you play influenced by the climate you live in?

   _____

   _____

6. How are the clothes you wear influenced by the climate of your area?

_____

_____

7. Do you want to move to a place in a different climate zone? If yes, why? Which climate? Why?

_____

_____

_____

## Charting

Complete the following chart in your notebook.

### CHART OF WORLD CLIMATE REGIONS

| Climate Region | Description | What Grows There | Areas or Countries Where the Climate is Found |
|---|---|---|---|
| Low Latitudes | | | |
| Tropical Rain Forest | | | |
| Savanna | | | |
| Desert | | | |
| Middle Latitudes | | | |
| Mediterranean | | | |
| Humid-Subtropical | | | |
| Marine | | | |
| Humid-Continental | | | |
| Continental Steppe | | | |
| Continental Deserts | | | |
| High Latitudes | | | |
| Taiga | | | |
| Tundra | | | |
| Vertical | | | |

## Chapter **12**

# Culture—Satisfying People's Basic Needs

**Reading for a Purpose**

1. What is meant by culture?
2. What is the relationship between geography and culture?
3. What is the relationship between culture and people's basic needs?
4. How are cultures alike and different?
5. What is the difference between race and culture?

## Knowing New Words

culture (KUL-chur)   The way of life of a group of people.
> There are people from many **cultures** living in New York City.

technology (tek-NAHL-uh-jee)   The use of science to make new things.
> Because of **technology** people can now travel in space.

ethnocentric (eth-noh-SEN-trik)   A feeling that one's way of life is the best and that everyone else should live the same way.
> Americans are often **ethnocentric** when they travel to foreign countries.

Can you think of three things that you cannot live without? If you are thinking of food, clothing, and shelter, you are right. These are people's basic needs. People all over the world meet their basic needs in different ways. Two things that affect how people meet their needs are the environment in which people live and the way people have chosen to use their environment. This chapter will explain how culture affects people's lives.

## Writing and Thinking

The pictures on page 67 show how people from some different places are meeting some of their needs. Study the pictures carefully. Then answer the questions that follow.

1. Which pictures have something to do with ruling oneself? _____

2. Which pictures have something to do with earning a living? _____

3. Which pictures have something to do with getting along with others? _____

4. Which human needs are being met in each picture?

   A. _____     B. _____

   C. _____     D. _____

5. What are two reasons why people satisfy their needs in different ways? Explain.

   _____

   _____

● After reading this chapter, come back to the answers you have written. Make any changes that you think will make the answers better.

# Geography Skills and Concepts

**1.** From the beginning of time geography has affected how people satisfied their needs for food, clothing, and shelter. How people meet their needs is part of what is called **culture**. How people work, the language they speak and the sports they play are all part of their culture. How people worship their god or gods, the government they have, and what they believe to be right and wrong are also part of culture. All these things and more make up a person's culture. Culture is the way of life of a group of people, everything that has to do with how they live.

**2.** A person's race is sometimes confused with his or her culture. There is a great difference. Culture is the way of life of a people. It is what the people have learned and decided to keep on doing. Race is a set of bodily traits shared by a group of people. Skin color is just one of these traits. The shape of one's eyes and the texture of one's hair are other racial traits. Racial groups share these characteristics. Racial traits, unlike culture, are not learned.

**3.** To learn about a people's culture you must also learn about their geography. The culture of a group depends a great deal on their surroundings or environment. Soil, climate, minerals, the kind of land surface, power resources—all of these are part of one's environment. Environment is one reason why people have different ways of living. To grow up in a desert is different from growing up in a rain forest. Environments throughout the world are not the same. Over the years people have found many ways of using their environment to help satisfy their needs. Some people fish, others hunt. Ways of living often differ even when the environment is the same. This is because things other than environment also affect how people live. When people do share the same patterns or ways of living, they are said to share the same culture.

**4.** Through science, people have been able to change their environment. Science has enabled people to make life more comfortable. Inventors put ideas and materials together to make things that did not exist before. The use of scientific knowledge to make and do new things is called **technology**. The United States has one of the most technological cultures in the world. There is very little that is not affected by technology.

**5.** There are some cultures that use less technology than the United States. There are many reasons for this. It may be because they do not have the knowledge. Perhaps they are unable to pay the costs of making or buying some needed items. This is the case in some parts of Asia, Africa, and the Middle East. There are some cultures where people refuse to use certain technology.

These people feel that some uses of technology are wrong or evil because of religious or other beliefs. The advantage of using technology is that you can be less dependent on your geography. The advantage of using less technology is that your life may be simpler.

6. People often believe that their culture is better than the culture of others. They may look down on those people who do things differently. The problem is made worse because people try to make others live as they do. The feeling that one way of life is better or superior to another is called ethnocentrism. The strong, or **ethnocentric**, feelings people have for their own culture is a world problem. One way of overcoming this problem is by getting people to know and understand each other. Technology has been helping to bring about this understanding. This has not always been easy.

7. Geography often prevents the spread of ideas from one culture to another. Oceans, mountains, deserts, and jungles all act to separate cultures. By using technology to build boats, tunnels, cars, and planes, people can now travel more easily. They can get to know and understand each other's cultures better. Perhaps in time there will be less ethnocentrism.

## Understanding What You Have Read

Choose the word or words that best complete each statement. Write the letter of your answer in the blank next to the number.

_____ 1. Culture is best defined as
a. a form of government   b. environment   c. a way of life

_____ 2. "I just can't understand how people in India permit their parents to choose their husbands for them." This quote is an example of
a. ethnocentrism   b. basic needs   c. technology

_____ 3. Cutting the grass with a power mower instead of a hand mower is an advance in
a. environment   b. technology   c. race

_____ 4. An American who is ethnocentric would say:
a. All countries should be democratic like we are.   b. American people are nice.
c. Our way of life is the best for us but not necessarily good for others.

## Critical Thinking

Read the items listed below. If you think the item has to do with race, place an *R* in the blank. If you think the item has to do with culture, place a *C* in the blank.

_____ 1. Fire

_____ 2. Time

_____ 3. The clothing a person wears

_____ 4. The language a person speaks

_____ 5. The shape of a person's head

_____ 6. The religion a person has

_____ 7. The kind of hair a person has

_____ 8. The government a person chooses

_____ 9. The color of a person's skin

_____ 10. The home a person lives in

_____ 11. The country a person comes from

_____ 12. The color of a person's eyes

_____ 13. The bone structure of a person

_____ 14. The games a person plays

_____ 15. The job a person has

## Making Inferences

Answer the following questions in the spaces provided.

1. Why do you think some countries have the same kind of culture?

_____

_____

2. Why do you think some countries have different kinds of culture?

_____

_____

3. Why do some countries that are far from each other have the same kinds of culture?

_____

_____

4. Do you think cultures in the world are becoming more alike or more different? Explain.

_____

_____

_____

## Essay

In your notebook, write the answer to the following question. How can technology be both good and bad for a person's culture?

# GEOGRAPHY ◆ HIGHLIGHTS

## Measuring Earthquakes

■ How do you measure earthquakes? When there has been a huge earthquake you will hear how large it was on the news. The earthquake will be measured on the Richter (RIK-tur) scale. The scale goes from 0 to 10. On that scale, an earthquake of below 2 will not be felt by people. At 4.5 there will be some damage from an earthquake. An earthquake that measures 6.5 is serious. A reading of above 8 promises real damage. Perhaps the greatest earthquake ever to hit the United States was the San Francisco earthquake of 1906. That earthquake is estimated at between 7.8 and 8.3 on the Richter scale. Over 500 people were killed. The fires the earthquake caused destroyed 4 square miles of the city.

# Chapter **13**

## What Makes Up the Physical Geography of an Area?

**Reading for a Purpose**

1. What makes up the geography of an area?
2. How do people use the natural resources of an area?

### Knowing New Words

**physical geography** (FIZ-ih-kul jee-AHG-ruh-fee)   The study of the earth's natural features.
  Every place on earth has its own distinct **physical geography**.

**biological resources** (by-uh-LAHJ-ih-kul REE-sohrs-is)   Resources that support life, such as plants and animals.
  Without **biological resources** people could not live.

**raw material** (RAW muh-TEER-ee-ul)   Something that is used to make a finished product.
  Cotton is a **raw material** that is used to make clothing.

───────────── ● ─────────────

Did you ever try to fit the pieces of a jigsaw puzzle together to make a whole picture? That is what you will do in this chapter. You have learned about most of the different "pieces" of geography. Now you will fit these pieces together.

### Writing and Thinking

Choose the term that best matches each part of the puzzle and label each. Then on page 72 define each term.

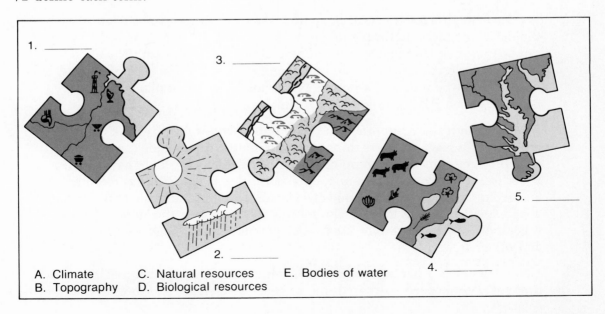

1. _____
2. _____
3. _____
4. _____
5. _____

A. Climate       C. Natural resources      E. Bodies of water
B. Topography    D. Biological resources

A. _____  D. _____

B. _____  E. _____

C. _____

● After reading this chapter, come back to the answers you have written. Make any changes you think will make your answers better.

# Geography Skills and Concepts

1. There are many forces that make up the geography of an area. These forces are what is known as **physical geography**. More simply, it is those things that are thought of as nature.

2. As you learned earlier, every place has its topography or landforms. There are four main kinds of landforms on the earth. These are mountains, hills, plateaus, and plains. Most of the land surface of the earth is made up of one of these four landforms.

3. There is much more water than land on the earth. In fact, if you divided the earth into four equal parts, three of those parts would be made up of water. There are the four oceans: the Pacific, the Atlantic, the Indian, and the Arctic. The parts of the Indian, Pacific, and Atlantic oceans near Antarctica are some times called the Antarctic Ocean. Then there are seas. These are large bodies of water almost completely surrounded by land. The Mediterranean, the Caribbean, the Arabian, and the Sea of Japan are all major seas. There are also rivers and lakes.

4. Each area has its own climate — that is, the kind of weather it has over a long period of time, year after year. Differences in climate mean differences in temperature, rainfall, and length of the growing season. All of these strongly influence the kinds of crops that are grown in an area. Housing and clothing are also strongly influenced by climate.

5. **Biological resources** are also part of the physical geography of an area. Biological resources are the plants and animals that an area can support. They can be found on land and in water. These life forms differ with the climate, type of soil, closeness to water, and topography of a place. For example, polar bears will not be found in a jungle. Nor would any jungle plants be found near the North Pole or in a desert, for that matter.

6. **Resources** are important in the development of an area. The natural resources of a place are those things found in nature that people can use. For example, uranium has been on earth much longer than people have been. *It became a resource only when people learned to use it*. Natural resources are used for making food, fuel, and **raw materials** for the production of finished goods. Every place has its natural resources. The waters of the land and wild vegetation were the first to be used. Then people learned to use soil, lumber, and minerals.

7. Water is a natural resource that most people accept without much thought. People need water to drink, to keep them clean, and to wash their

food. A city of one million people could use as much as 50 million gallons of water a day! People also need water for growing crops. In areas where there is not enough rainfall people must irrigate, or bring water to the dry areas. Water also gives people a means of travel and of carrying goods. It is also an important source of power. Power plants near rivers and waterfalls use water to turn machines that then produce electricity. This is called hydroelectricity.

*The Aswan Dam in Egypt not only produces electric power but it also provides water for irrigation. Why is irrigation important in this region?*

8. The soil that covers the earth is a valuable resource. People need fertile soil in order to grow crops. The topsoil throughout the world is usually only about eight inches deep. This thin layer of topsoil is made up mainly of minerals and living things. The topsoil contains plants and insects as well as water, air, and minerals. The minerals are called nutrients. As long as the nutrients remain, the land is useful for growing crops.

9. Forests are one of the valuable resources of the world. They still cover about one-fifth of the earth's surface. Most of the large forests are found in the northern climate zones such as Canada, Alaska, Norway, Sweden, Finland, and Siberia. Other large forests are found in rain-forest regions such as South America, central Africa, and Southeast Asia. Trees help keep the soil on steep hillsides from being washed away. Forests also provide a home for wildlife and a place of beauty and fun for millions of people. People have found many other uses for trees. Homes, fuel, newsprint, and turpentine are a few of the products from forests.

10. Mineral resources are not as important as soils, water, and vegetation in supporting life. However, they are very important for modern living. Minerals are used as raw materials. They are used to make finished goods such as cars, dishes, clothing, and computers. Some minerals, such as coal, oil, and natural gas, are used for fuels. They give people heat, light, and power for their homes.

11. As you study geography you will learn more about natural resources. Natural resources differ from region to region throughout the world. People make use of natural resources in different ways. Many of the great resources are being used up. When people come to an area they change it. Sometimes they change it for the better and sometimes for the worse.

## Categorizing

**1.** Write each of the following words under the category to which it belongs. Some items can go into more than one category. Then think of two more items to add to each category.

| | | | |
|---|---|---|---|
| sheep | winter | ocean plants | snow |
| cotton | 72 degrees | fish | iron |
| wheat | 25 inches of rainfall | cows | lead |
| coal | fall | Atlantic Ocean | trees |
| Nevada desert | oil | Rocky Mountains | sand |
| Grand Canyon | fruit trees | birds | |

| Climate | Topography | Biological Resources | Mineral Resources | Waterways | Raw Materials |
|---------|-----------|---------------------|-------------------|-----------|---------------|
| | | | | | |
| | | | | | |
| | | | | | |
| | | | | | |
| | | | | | |
| | | | | | |
| | | | | | |
| | | | | | |
| | | | | | |

**2.** In your notebook, create an imaginary place that includes all the things mentioned in this chapter. It has to be a place that is untouched by humans. Then list the resources that are useless because there are no people in this place.

# GEOGRAPHY HIGHLIGHTS

## The Disappearing Rain Forests

■ Will the rain forests disappear? The plants and trees of the tropical rain forest are among the fastest-growing plants in the world. But people are cutting down the rain forest for lumber and to grow crops. By some estimates, as much as 25 acres of rain forest are being cut down every minute! Today there are around 40,000 square miles of rain forest in the world, about one-half of what there was in 1900. By the year 2000, another 12 percent will be gone. At that rate, there will be no rain forests left in the world by the year 2100.

# Chapter **14**

## People and Places

### Reading for a Purpose

1. How do cities develop?
2. What makes a city successful?
3. What kinds of changes do people make to the environment?

### Knowing New Words

crossroads (KROS-rohds)   A place where two or more roads cross.
    A good place for a business is at a **crossroads**.

harmony (HAR-muh-nee)   To be at peace with someone or something.
    People want to live in **harmony** with their neighbors.

---

Large numbers of people stay in certain places for very good reasons. In Chapter 13 you learned about physical geography and environment. Different features of physical geography attract people to them. It might be the climate or certain natural resources that make a place special. People come to a place in order to satisfy their needs. Sometimes the needs are simply for food, clothing, and shelter. It might also be for the freedom of speech, opportunity, or religion. For whatever reasons people choose a particular place to live, when they get there they make changes. This chapter will explain some reasons why cities developed where they did and the changes people make to areas.

---

### Writing and Thinking

Study the cartoon. Then make the following additions to the cartoon.

1. Label the forces of physical geography that attract people to a place.
2. Label the changes people make to a place that attract other people.

● After reading this chapter, come back to the answers you have written. Make any changes that you think will make your answers better.

**1.** People moving into a place tend to change it in order to meet their needs. They use their technology to change the environment. Sometimes, changes in the environment attract even more people to a place. These changes might include railroad centers, gold mines, or seats of government. Sometimes the rules for a place, such as religious freedom, attract more people. As large numbers of people begin to live in one area, a city is begun. It is while building cities that people make the greatest changes in the environment. But what makes a city successful?

**2.** Geographical location is an important factor in the growth of cities. A person will start a business at a place where there will be the most customers. And so it is with cities. Some early settlements grew into large cities. Others did not. The location of a settlement is very often the main reason for its growth. The better the location, the more likely it is that the city will grow. The earliest cities were located in the river valleys of Asia and Africa. In these fertile valleys, people were able to grow crops, and the rivers gave them easy transportation. Early towns developed near **crossroads** where merchants met, along rivers, and near good harbors.

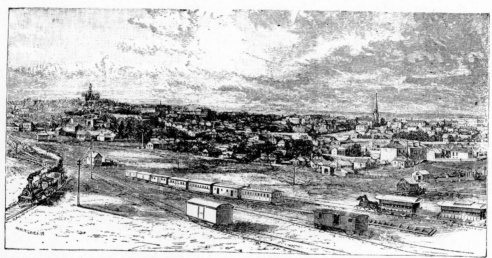

*Omaha, Nebraska, in 1876. What attracted people to this area?*

**3.** Throughout history, settlements have grown where one kind of transportation ended and another began. At these places, goods have to be unloaded and loaded. People stop for a rest. They get supplies to continue their journey. When early railroad tracks were laid in the western United States, settlements grew where the railroad line ended. Omaha, Nebraska, and Topeka, Kansas, are examples of these railroad cities. Such cities also developed where rivers and oceans met. At New Orleans, Louisiana, goods were unloaded from riverboats and loaded onto oceangoing ships. Locate these cities on the map on page 77. Can you locate any other railroad cities?

**4.** Most of the world's large cities started as small seaports, or river ports. As more goods were shipped through these cities, they grew. By 1860, there were nine cities in the United States with 100,000 people. Six of these were

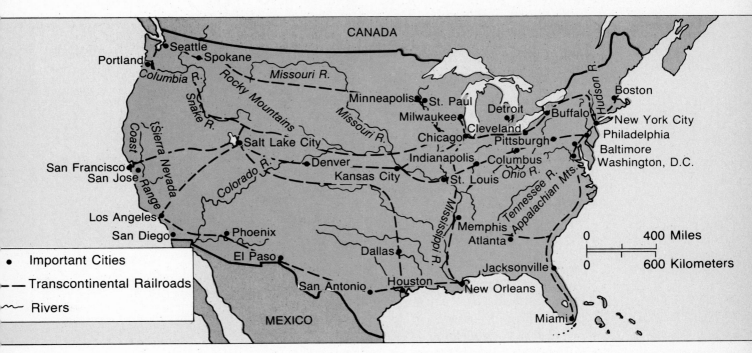

seaports; the other three were river ports. Large cities such as Chicago and Cleveland also began on lakes. Another good place to start a city was near a source for water power. Many New England and southern towns used the waterfalls of swift-flowing streams as water power to run their mills. Locate the seaport or river port cities on the map.

**5.** The mining of valuable minerals has helped the growth of other cities. Cities developed near mineral deposits because of the large number of miners that were needed. Pittsburgh, Pennsylvania, and Birmingham, Alabama, are examples of steel centers. This is because they are located near iron ore and coal deposits. The gold rush of 1849 turned San Francisco into a city of 50,000 people within a few months. Favorable climate has caused the growth of cities, too. The cities in Florida and California are among the fastest-growing in the United States.

**6.** Where people live can be shown on a map. Maps that show the number of people living in an area are called population density maps. The more people living in a region, the more dense its population. Regions that have few people are said to have a sparse, or small, population density.

**7.** Wherever people have settled in the world, they have changed their environment. The greatest changes are made in cities. The fewest changes are made in the countryside. Some of these changes are the same or nearly the same throughout the world. Many of the changes are different from one culture to another.

**8.** Some people have made only slight changes in the environment. There are many reasons for this. The people may not have the advanced technology needed to change the environment. They may feel it is wrong to change nature. Thus they try to live in close **harmony** with nature. Other people have almost totally changed their natural environment. They use technology to create their own environment. They try to create a place that meets their needs without depending on nature.

## Understanding What You Have Read

Choose the word or words that best complete each statement. Write the letter of your answer in the blank next to the number.

_____ 1. People make the greatest change in the environment when they
a. sail boats   b. build cities   c. grow crops

_____ 2. People change their environment through
a. technology   b. geography   c. resources

_____ 3. The location of a settlement is often the reason for its
a. crossroads   b. technology   c. growth

_____ 4. Early towns developed near
a. crossroads   b. other towns   c. basic needs

_____ 5. Most early cities developed near all of the following *except*
a. deserts   b. rivers   c. railroad lines

_____ 6. Swift-flowing streams were an important source of
a. money   b. technology   c. water power

_____ 7. The following is a part of physical geography
a. climate   b. needs   c. technology

_____ 8. Which is not important to the success of early cities?
a. growth   b. geography   c. recreational activities

## Critical Thinking

In the space provided explain the following:
Physical geography + human additions = a place in the world today.

_____

_____

_____

## Interpreting a Chart

Many American Indians (Native Americans) lived where modern Americans live today. They, however, did not change the physical geography as much as the early European settlers or as much as the modern Americans have. The changes they did make were different. Use the chart to answer the questions that follow and give explanations for the differences.

| Group | Cultural Ideas of Right and Wrong | Technology | Physical Geography |
|---|---|---|---|
| American Indian | No idea of land ownership. Land was free for all. All nature is living and like humans, all elements have spirits. It is good to be as one with nature. | Stone tools Fire | Woodlands in the eastern United States Rivers, streams, and some clearings |
| Early European Settlers | Land is wealth. Gifts of nature are for the use of people. | Metal tools such as saws, plows. Domesticated animals | Woodlands in the eastern United States Rivers, streams, and some clearings. |

1. Describe two ways in which the Indians and the settlers used the land differently. Explain why.

   _____

   _____

   _____

2. Which group was more likely to use up the land's fertility and move on? Why?

   _____

   _____

3. Which group was less likely to pollute the waters? Why?

   _____

   _____

4. Which group was more likely to change the physical environment for physical comfort?

   _____

   _____

   _____

# GEOGRAPHY HIGHLIGHTS

## Population and Climate

■ Are climate and population related? You have been reading about climate and its importance to people. But can climate have something to do with population? Yes! People will settle where the climate best meets their needs. So there is a direct relationship between climate and population. Most of the world's population lives in the humid subtropical climate zone.

# Chapter 15

# Making Changes to Environment: Does It Improve Life?

## Reading for a Purpose

1. How much does modern technology affect people's everyday lives?
2. What dangers do people face as a result of technology?

## Knowing New Words

survive (sur-VYV)   To remain alive.
>    If properly trained and equipped, people have the ability to **survive** in the jungles, deserts, and polar regions.

industrial (in-DUS-tree-ul)   Having to do with making things in factories by machines.
>    The United States is an **industrial** country with millions of factories.

source (SOHRS)   Any thing or place from which something comes.
>    The **source** of our daylight is the sun.

pollution (puh-LOO-shun)   Dirt, especially in the air or water.
>    Companies and people should work to clean up the **pollution** in our air.

---

People have **survived** on earth because they have been able to change their environment. Early men and women learned to use nature's "gifts" as tools. With these tools, they could hunt, protect themselves, and build shelters. They learned to plant crops, train animals, and change nature's products into new products. Today the world is greatly affected by technology. This has given people many comforts and freedoms. Technology has, however, brought people many unexpected problems. Some of these problems could threaten their way of life. This chapter focuses on how much the world has been changed.

---

## Writing and Thinking

List the items you see in the picture that were created out of nature by modern technology. Try to tell how each was created or discovered. Use the chart on page 81 to write your answers.

| Item Created from Nature by Technology | How It Was Created or Discovered |
|---|---|
| | |

In the following space, write what you think is the main idea of this picture.

_____

_____

_____

_____

_____

● After reading this chapter, come back to the answers you have written. Make any changes you think will make your answers better.

## Geography Skills and Concepts

1. Air, water, forests, soil, metals, and minerals are all natural resources. These resources are part of the reason for the growth in the number of people in the world. Human resources are another. People are human resources. People have used natural resources to make their lives better. This has been done by inventing and using machines.

2. The greatest change in the way people use natural resources took place in the 17th and 18th centuries. This change was called the **Industrial** Revolution. A revolution is the kind of change that brings about a new way of life for many people. During the Industrial Revolution, machines were invented to make goods. Many goods once made by hand in the home were now made by machines in factories. New kinds of power were found to run these machines. Steam, made by burning coal, was one kind of new power.

3. The factories needed raw materials from which to make the goods. For example, coal and iron ore were used to make steel. As factories grew there were jobs for many people. Thousands of people left their farms and moved near the factories. As time went on, more and different products were invented, more businesses and jobs were created, and cities grew larger.

4. New machines were invented for use on the farms as well. As a result, fewer farmers were needed to grow crops. They were able to feed people throughout the nation and the world. In addition to crops for daily living they grew cash crops such as tobacco and cotton. Cash crops, or money crops, are products that could be grown and sold at a profit. Farms, just as factories, became big businesses.

5. Inventions continued to be made. Railroads took the place of horse-drawn carriages. Steamships replaced the great sailing ships. Other **sources** of power were found, such as oil and atomic energy. Automobiles and airplanes were invented. Goods could be carried swiftly and cheaply almost anywhere in the world. The invention of the telephone, telegraph, radio, and television made it possible for people all over the world to communicate with each other.

6. Today countries like the United States, Great Britain, Canada, Japan, West Germany, France, and the Soviet Union are all industrial nations. The people of these and other countries like them make up about one-third of the world. Most of these people live well. They have enough food and water for their needs. And they have money for many of the goods and services they need. But there are many problems as well.

7. One of the problems is **pollution**. The pollution of the air is a serious health problem. Dirt and loose soil are blown into the air by the wind. Gas and chemicals are blown into the air by automobiles, incinerators, factories, refineries, and power plants. A mass of warm air over a city can trap dirty air. The result is smog, a foglike smoke. Dirty air damages trees. It can peel paint on a house. It can eat away at brick and stone. Most of all, it harms people. Killer smogs have hit cities like London and New York. People have difficulty breathing when the smog is very bad. Those with illnesses of the heart and lungs are in special danger. As the need for more power and more products increases, the air gets more and more polluted.

8. People cannot live without water any more than they can live without air. Each person in the United States uses 87 gallons of water per day. Farmers need water. Factories use great amounts of water. For example, it takes 100,000 gallons of water to make one automobile. To refine one barrel of oil, 700 gallons of water are needed. Yet people have allowed the water systems to be damaged by pollution. People and factories dump their wastes into the water. Nearly all rivers in the United States have been polluted in some way.

9. A growing concern to many countries is "acid rain." The chemical pollutants that are getting into the air are being changed to acid and coming back to earth in the rain. This is causing many problems. The water in many lakes has fewer fish. Trees are not growing to their full height. Some soils are being ruined. In the United States this is fast becoming a national problem.

10. At one time people believed that there was no end to the supplies of natural resources. However, in recent years people have begun to realize that many of these resources are almost gone. The United States, for example, has used up much of its rich deposits of iron ore. In fact, modern Americans have used as much coal, oil, and iron ore as all the people that came before them. Even now, the United States is using as much as the rest of the world combined. People must all work to save these resources.

## Interpreting Cartoons

In the balloons, write what you think the bird and the fish are saying to each other.

## Understanding What You Have Read

Read the following statements. Explain each statement and tell what world problem is being referred to.

1. Our lungs tell the story: People who spend their lives in the mountains have pink lungs; the lungs of city dwellers are as black as coal.

2. On a clear day you can see your toes.

3. Fishing in the future will be easier than ever. Just take the dead fish off the top of the water.

4. We know that, everything else aside, pollution stinks.

5. The smog was so thick in the morning, a helicopter stopped and the pilot asked the way to the airport.

## Interpreting a Pictograph

Answer the following questions about the pictograph.

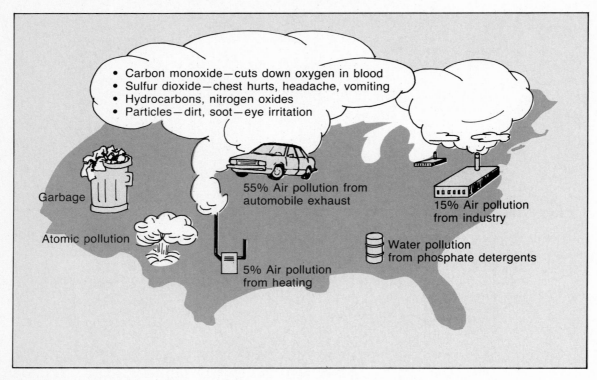

1. Which pollutant hurts the eyes?

   _____

2. What causes the greatest amount of air pollution?

   _____

3. In addition to sewage and factory wastes, how can waters be polluted?

   _____

   _____

4. Which pollutant shown gives off radioactive wastes?

   _____

5. What is the second-worst pollutant of the air?

   _____

6. Which type of air pollution do you think is most dangerous to your health? Why?

   _____

   _____

   _____

7. Can you think of any other way that your way of life is in danger because of pollution?

   _____

   _____

   _____

# Unit 4 Review

## Building Your Vocabulary

Find each of the following words in the puzzle. When you find the word, circle it. Then, in the space next to each word in the list, write how the word is related to the geography of a place.

```
E  E  N  V  I  R  O  N  M  E  N  T  V
V  T  E  M  H  T  P  N  J  S  L  E  L
L  K  H  A  R  M  O  N  Y  L  R  C  S
U  R  U  N  C  I  D  S  C  S  B  H  D
I  E  H  P  O  L  L  U  T  I  O  N  A
N  S  U  H  E  C  Z  P  R  C  Q  O  O
E  O  A  D  A  U  E  Z  K  A  Y  L  R
I  U  T  S  O  L  S  N  L  H  Y  O  S
T  R  S  F  N  T  A  Q  T  G  X  G  S
V  C  D  U  G  U  P  A  O  R  B  Y  O
G  E  O  R  I  R  O  J  D  S  I  F  R
M  G  O  W  E  E  G  X  T  I  O  C  C
I  N  D  U  S  T  R  I  A  L  A  W  A
```

culture _____

environment _____

technology _____

ethnocentric _____

resource _____

crossroads _____

harmony _____

industrial _____

pollution _____

# Critical Thinking: Making Inferences

Read the following geographical descriptions of three places. Some information is also included about the technology of the people living there. Then read the statements in the chart. Complete the chart to show where each speaker comes from. Put a check in the box that best relates to each speaker.

*Description of Place "A":*

Mostly plains and plateaus. Less than 10 inches of rain a year fall in most areas. Three major rivers. Large deposits of petroleum. Located on or near large waterways that connect it to major countries of the world. THE CULTURE DOES NOT CREATE A HIGH LEVEL OF TECHNOLOGY.

*Description of Place "B":*

This is an area made up of many islands. Eighty-five percent of the land is mountainous. On and off throughout the year heavy rains fall. Some forest and mineral resources. Climate is influenced by ocean currents. THE CULTURE CREATES A VERY HIGH LEVEL OF TECHNOLOGY.

*Description of Place "C":*

People were kept apart from the rest of the mainland by mountains and water. Lots of coastline. Many natural barriers inside the country, such as deserts, plateaus, and mountains. Dependent on rains brought at certain times each year. A few major rivers that are fed by streams from the mountains. The country was once defeated and ruled by a foreign power. THE CULTURE IS GROWING IN ITS ABILITY TO PRODUCE HIGH LEVELS OF TECHNOLOGY.

| *Speaker #* | *Place "A"* | *Place "B"* | *Place "C"* | *Not Enough Information to Decide* |
|---|---|---|---|---|
| 1. I come from a place where irrigation is possible. | | | | |
| 2. Many different languages are spoken in my country. | | | | |
| 3. From 1640 to 1850 our leaders kept us apart from the rest of the world. If you think about it, it wasn't too hard to do. | | | | |
| 4. We have few cows because there isn't enough land on which to graze them. | | | | |
| 5. We have become successful in today's world by buying the natural resources that we don't have and using them to make products that the rest of the world can use. | | | | |

| Speaker # | Place "A" | Place "B" | Place "C" | Not Enough Information to Decide |
|---|---|---|---|---|
| **6.** We trade an important resource for goods that we currently are unable to make ourselves. | | | | |
| **7.** We trade a lot with other countries by sea. | | | | |
| **8.** Many people go hungry and even starve if the rains do not come on time to water the seeds we have planted. | | | | |
| **9.** We are interested in learning new technology. | | | | |
| **10.** We have a strong government. | | | | |

## Using Geography

Study this map of an imaginary country. Then answer the questions about it on page 88. Write the letter of your answer in the blank next to each number.

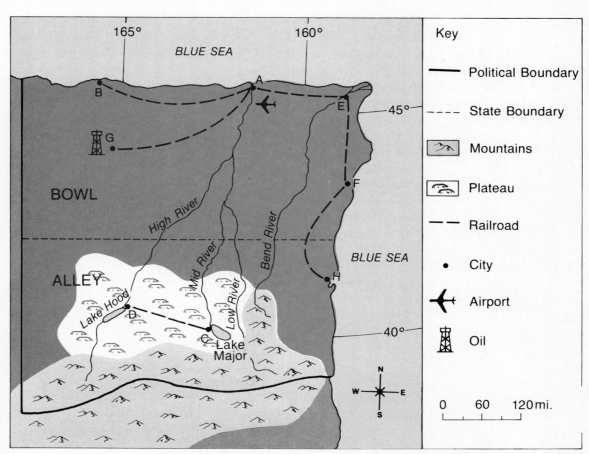

Use the map on page 87 to answer these questions.

_____ 1. Which city is probably the busiest railroad center?
a. City A   b. City B   c. City C

_____ 2. In which general direction are all of the rivers flowing?
a. north   b. south   c. west

_____ 3. What is located about 30 miles southeast of A?
a. oil wells   b. mountains   c. an airport

_____ 4. Which state has the greatest total population?
a. Bowl   b. Alley   c. not enough information to tell

_____ 5. Why do you think City G is located where it is?
a. There is lots of water nearby.   b. Oil was discovered there.
c. The railroad went there.

_____ 6. Why do you think Cities D and C are located where they are?
a. They are near lakes.   b. It is warmer than the rest of the country.
c. The railroad went there.

_____ 7. Which geographical features probably helped to unite the people of this country?
a. the railroads   b. the seas   c. the rivers

_____ 8. Why do you think the people in this country settled here?
a. because of the water   b. because oil was here
c. because the temperature is most comfortable

_____ 9. Where is there probably the most pollution in this country?
a. near City A   b. near City E   c. near City C

_____ 10. Which people in this country probably use more technology in their everyday lives?
a. the people living along the riverbanks
b. the people living in the state of Bowl
c. the people living in the state of Alley

## Chapter **16**

# How Are Natural Resources Valued?

**Reading for a Purpose**

1. What are natural resources?
2. What is internationalism?
3. How are the prices of natural resources set?

## Knowing New Words

natural resources (NACH-uh-rul REE-sors-is)   Materials found in nature that people use.
  Our rich farmlands are an important **natural resource** to America.

import (im-POHRT)   To bring into a country.
  The United States **imports** many products from Japan.

internationalism (in-tur-NASH-shun-nul-iz-um)   The process of something being shared or
  used by two or more nations.
  Young people all over the world wear jeans; it is a sign of **internationalism** among
    the young.

———————●———————

  **Natural resources** are found all over the world. They come in many forms, and some are more valuable than others. Natural resources are not evenly distributed, however. What is a valuable resource to one country may not be valuable to another. This depends on the need a country has for the resource. But nations trade natural resources with each other. In this way a country can meet its own needs while helping others to meet theirs.

## Writing and Thinking

  Study the cartoon carefully. Then answer the questions that follow.

Use the cartoon on page 89 to answer the questions.

1. What do you think natural resources are?

   _____

   _____

2. Why do you think natural resources are important to a country?

   _____

   _____

3. Why do you think that some countries have more to sell than others?

   _____

   _____

4. Why do you think that some countries need to buy more than others?

   _____

   _____

5. Do you think that all natural resources are worth the same amount of money? Do you think this affects how the world exchanges them?

   _____

   _____

● After reading this chapter, come back to the answers you have written. Make any changes that you think will make the answers better.

# Geography Skills and Concepts

1. Can you imagine throwing oil away because you do not want it? Back in the 1840s, oil was not needed very much in the United States. This changed as the United States began to use oil for many things. The United States needed more and more oil, so it became very valuable. The United States began buying oil from countries that had a large supply, mainly from the Middle East. When the countries in the Middle East stopped shipping oil to the United States in the 1970s, the price rose. People had to pay very high prices for oil that was once thought to be useless.

*The discovery of offshore oil in the North Sea has changed the United Kingdom from an oil-importing nation to an oil-exporting nation. How has this helped the United Kingdom's economy?*

2. Oil is an example of a natural resource. Natural resources are materials found in nature that people can use. Natural resources come in many different forms and have many different values. A nation's income is largely determined by the value of its natural resources. The Middle East has always had oil. But so did many other countries. The Middle East has always sold oil, but it did not make the Arab countries rich. However, when other countries began to need oil from the Middle East, the price of oil suddenly rose. The sale of that natural resource made the Arab countries rich.

3. Japan is a country rich in people, but it has few natural resources. It must **import**, or bring into the country, almost all of its oil. It needs to import food, timber, metal, machinery, and equipment. Yet Japan is one of the richest countries on earth. How can that be? Japan buys raw, or unprocessed, natural resources. The Japanese then manufacture goods from the raw natural resource. For example, they import iron. They use the iron to make steel. They **export** the cars they make from the steel. The Japanese then sell these cars to other countries for more than it cost to make them from the raw natural resources they imported. In this way, they make money even though their resources are few.

4. Chad is also a country with few natural resources. It must import oil, food, machines, and technology. Its people eat most of the products they grow, so there is little food to sell to other countries. But Chad does sell some cotton and a few cattle. Because Chad has few natural resources to sell, it is among the poorest countries on earth. It has no valuable resource whose price it can raise to make its people rich.

5. There are many natural resources that are in high demand worldwide. This has led to the **internationalism** of demand, or the process of natural resources being sought by several countries at once. If there are many places on earth where the natural resource is found, its price may stay the same. But if a resource is suddenly needed and its supply is small, then the price will rise.

6. What is a natural resource worth? It is worth whatever people will pay for it. The value of a natural resource comes from its use, its supply, and the need or demand for it. In the Sahara, water is a valuable natural resource with a high price because it is hard to find there. In Canada there is plenty of water, so it has almost no value when it is sold. However, diamonds are rare around the world and many people want them, so they are valuable as a natural resource worldwide.

## Understanding What You Have Read

Write *T* next to each statement that is true. Write *F* next to each statement that is false. Then change each false statement to make it true.

_____ 1. Natural resources are materials found in nature that people can use.

_____ 2. People cannot be thought of as a natural resource.

_____ **3.** Natural resources are found evenly distributed throughout the world.

_____

_____

_____ **4.** The value of a natural resource comes from how much of it there is and from nothing else.

_____

_____

_____ **5.** It is possible for a natural resource to be valuable at one time in history and not valuable at another.

_____

_____

_____ **6.** The worldwide demand for some natural resources has led to the internationalism of demand.

_____

_____

## Reading a Natural Resources Map

This map shows the natural resources of oil, gas, coal, and certain minerals that are found in the United States. Study the map carefully. Then answer the questions that follow.

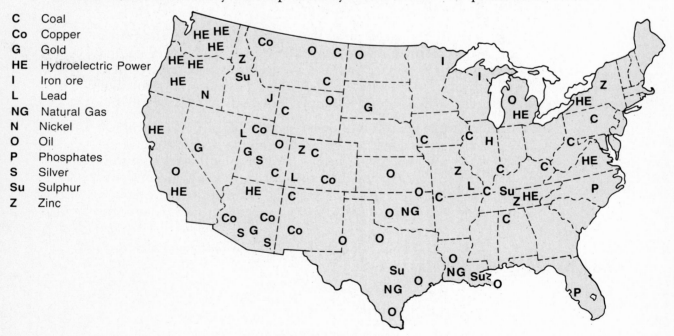

| | |
|---|---|
| **C** | Coal |
| **Co** | Copper |
| **G** | Gold |
| **HE** | Hydroelectric Power |
| **I** | Iron ore |
| **L** | Lead |
| **NG** | Natural Gas |
| **N** | Nickel |
| **O** | Oil |
| **P** | Phosphates |
| **S** | Silver |
| **Su** | Sulphur |
| **Z** | Zinc |

1. The United States has coal, oil, and natural gas resources. These are all important types of fuel. In how many states are these things found?

_____

2. To which states could you go if you were going to mine for both gold and silver? (Use the map on page 108 if you need help with state locations.)

_____

3. Phosphates are important natural resources for making fertilizer. Fertilizer is an important part of the U.S. farming economy, and the United States is the "breadbasket of the world" as a farming nation. Where would you go to mine for phosphates?

_____

_____

4. In what areas are oil-producing fields found?

_____

_____

5. Where are gas-producing fields found?

_____

_____

6. Bauxite is a mineral that is used in making aluminum. The United States uses a lot of aluminum. Do you think it imports or exports bauxite? Explain your answer.

_____

_____

_____

7. Hydroelectricity is electric power that is made from falling water. On this map does hydroelectricity seem to be an important natural resource that Americans have learned to use? In what type of topography would you expect a hydroelectric plant to be found?

_____

_____

_____

8. Would you expect the United States to import or export metals? Explain your answer.

_____

_____

_____

## Using What You Know

Below is a newspaper headline. Write a story that would go with the headline. Tell what happened, what will happen to the price of zinc, and what will happen to the price of gold. Explain your reasoning in the story, and use the natural resource map to help you.

### U.S. Scientist Announces Process for Making Gold Out of Zinc

_____

_____

_____

_____

_____

_____

# Chapter 17

## What Does It Mean to Be Interdependent?

### Reading for a Purpose

1. What is interdependence?
2. How does cultural diffusion affect the world?
3. What is meant by a globe with three worlds?

### Knowing New Words

**interdependent** (in-tur-dih-PEN-dunt)    Having to do with people of different cultures needing things from other cultures.
We live in an **interdependent** world.

**cultural diffusion** (KUL-chur-ul dif-YOO-zhun)    The spread of ideas from one culture into others.
Young people around the world listening to rock music is a sign of **cultural diffusion**.

**self-sufficient** (SELF-suf-FISH-unt)    Not in need of anyone or anything else.
There are few, if any, **self-sufficient** cultures in the world today.

**political** (puh-LIT-ih-kul)    Having to do with the government or how people are ruled.
There are **political** differences between the United States and the Soviet Union.

———————— ● ————————

The world's resources are sent everywhere in exchange for other products or materials. The natural resources on earth are unevenly distributed. Therefore, countries must trade with each other to get the resources they need. This has made an **interdependent** world. Along with trade, cultures exchange their ideas, fashions, and thinking. This has brought about **cultural diffusion**.

---

### Writing and Thinking

Study the cartoon carefully. Then answer the questions on page 95.

1. What types of things are the countries of the world trading?

_____

_____

_____

2. Why do you think that the countries of the world need to trade with each other?

_____

_____

_____

3. What do you think that the world meant by "my world is interdependent"? Explain your answer.

_____

_____

_____

4. What do you think cultural diffusion is? Can you cite any examples from the cartoon to support your explanation?

_____

_____

_____

● After reading this chapter, come back to the answers you have written. Make any changes that you think will make the answers better.

## Geography Skills and Concepts

1. You sit down to eat a slice of pizza that is loaded with all kinds of toppings. You might not realize this, but the world is in front of you. The wheat in the pizza dough may have come from the American Midwest, or it may have come from Argentina or Italy. The tomatoes in the sauce may have been grown in California or Florida, or they may have come from Brazil. The Jalapeño (hah-luh-PAYN-yoh) peppers probably came from Mexico. The cheese could be American, Italian, or Canadian. The anchovies probably came from the Mediterranean Sea. The whole world sits on your plate.

2. The pizza is an example of interdependence, how people of different cultures need or want things from other cultures. The word *interdependence* is easy to analyze: *inter* means "between or among" and *dependence* means "depending, or counting, upon." Today people live in an interdependent world. In the case of the pizza, the idea for it was Italian. The food for it came from many countries. Both the idea of the food and the items in the pizza came from trading and sharing among people of various countries. The idea of pizza is an example of cultural diffusion—the idea of one culture showing up in other cultures. Notice how many restaurants you see in America that feature the foods of other cultures and you will see cultural diffusion at work.

3. Is there a group of people that is not interdependent? That is not likely. A group that does not need materials, ideas, or help from some other group is called self-sufficient. Perhaps somewhere in the world's rain forests there may be small bands of people who do not trade with others and who are self-sufficient. Are they better off? They do not have modern medicines. They do not have modern technology or varied crops. They have only their ideas, their inventions, and their own answers to problems. They do not benefit from the ideas and resources of others.

4. Do people today live in a world that seems to be getting bigger because of the greater information they have about each other and the world's resources? Or do people today live in a world that seems to be getting smaller because cultural diffusion is making the different cultures and people more alike? People today are living in both worlds.

5. The world is getting bigger because the more people share their ideas, their answers to problems, and their needs, the more there is for the world to draw from. An American doctor, Jonas Salk, found a way to keep children from getting polio, a terrible illness. Children all over the world were dying and being injured by polio. Dr. Salk's medicine is now given to children in almost every country of the world. That is cultural diffusion making life better for everyone.

6. Cultural diffusion and interdependence gave Henry Ford an important place in history. He was the first to manufacture automobiles on an assembly line. Learning from Ford, the Japanese now have factories in which robots do all the work of putting the automobile frames together without anyone helping them! Two ideas, the automobile and the assembly line, and the creative thinking of people in many countries make the automobile an example of how cultural diffusion and interdependence are helping people to grow.

7. The world also seems to be getting smaller. This does not mean that the real size of the world has changed; it just means that people are able to get together faster, to exchange ideas and products. You can watch the world news to see this in action. The reporters talk to each other as if they were in the same room, yet they can be a hemisphere apart. The food in the grocery store is another example. The fresh fish caught in the morning off the Maine coast can be dinner in Los Angeles that evening. Also, technology allows people to see and talk to each other across the miles as if there were no distance. It also allows resources to be taken where the demand is. All of this makes the world seem smaller.

8. You may have heard that there are three worlds on earth. When this is said, people are talking about **political** worlds, or groupings of nations based on how they are governed. The two you are probably most familiar with are the Free World and the Communist World. The Free World is made up mostly of the world's democracies (dih-MOK-ruh-sees), countries where people vote for their government and decide how they are to be ruled. In the Communist World the government owns the resources and factories, and people have little voice in the rules they live by. The Soviet Union is the leader of the Communist World. The United States is the leader of the Free World. The Third World is made up of many of the developing or poor nations of the world. Some have limited resources, and they all have great needs. They are called the Third World because they are not linked to either of the other two groups and lack the power of the other political worlds.

## Understanding What You Have Read

Write *T* next to each statement that is true. Write *F* next to each statement that is false. Then change each false statement to make it true.

_____ 1. When people learn about and share things in each other's cultures this is called interdependence.

_____

_____ 2. An example of cultural diffusion would be a student in China listening to rock music on the way to class.

_____

_____ 3. A group of people who do not share ideas or trade with anyone else and who solve their own problems is called self-sufficient.

_____

_____ 4. Today people live in a bigger world because technology makes distance seem unimportant when people study each other.

_____

_____ 5. There is only one political world, made up of all the world's nations.

_____

_____

## Interpreting Pictures

Study the two pictures. The one on the left is from New York City. The one on the right is from Tokyo, Japan. In both pictures, look for examples of cultural diffusion and circle them. Then write down what you think both pictures tell you about interdependence and cultural diffusion.

## Using What You Know

Read the menu carefully. Then answer the questions that follow.

---

### The Family Restaurant Menu

1. **Chinese chicken:** A delicious blend of old China. Mandarin oranges from Taiwan, water chestnuts from Beijing smothered in a Spanish-style sauce, settled on a bed of Tokyo rice.

2. **Chicken à la king:** Plump, British-breaded chicken cooked as only the French can. Served with a wine sauce on a light Danish pastry.

3. **Chicken Kiev:** A favorite of the Ukraine. Tender breasts of Romanoff chicken soaked in California wine, drowned in Swiss and mozzarella cheeses, and stuffed with herb bread from the Indies.

4. **Italian spaghetti:** You'd never know that spaghetti came from China originally with this Italian favorite. The freshest Florida vegetables and blushing Brazilian tomatoes make the perfect sauce for our durum wheat pasta. Sprinkled with Wisconsin cheese and served with French rolls.

5. **All-American hot dog:** All-natural, low-fat beef from Costa Rica. Snuggled into a chewy Russian roll, spiced with British horseradish and Spanish onion, it is topped with mustard that has a French tang.

6. **Beef teriyaki:** The Oriental touch to a great favorite. American beef cubed and stir-fried in a wok, with just a touch of soy sauce and rice wine. This dish rests on a bed of white South American rice.

Finish your meal with mountain-grown Kenya coffee or Canadian fruit!

---

1. Circle each item that is an example of cultural diffusion.
2. How does this menu demonstrate interdependence? Use examples from the menu to support your point.

_____

_____

3. How would the menu be different if it were a menu from a self-sufficient society? What would you have for dinner?

_____

_____

4. What parts of the menu come from each of the three worlds?

_____

_____

_____

_____

## Reading a Chart

Here are some facts about three countries. One, the United Kingdom, is a democratic industrialized nation. Another, Hungary, is an industrialized Communist country. The third, Senegal, is a developing country. Study the economic information about each country. Then answer the questions that follow.

| | United Kingdom | Hungary | Senegal |
|---|---|---|---|
| Gross Domestic Product | $458 billion (1983) | $18.6 billion (1983) | $2.3 billion (1982) |
| Per Capita Income (1983) | $9,180 | $2,150 | $440 |
| Industries | steel, metals, cars, ship-building, banking, in-surance, textiles, clothing, electronics, air-craft, machinery | iron and steel, machinery, medicines, cars, communications equipment, milling | food processing, fishing |
| Chief Crops | grains, sugar beets, fruits, vegetables | grains, vegetables, fruits, grapes | peanuts, millet, rice |
| Minerals | coal, tin, oil, gas, iron, limestone, salt, clay, chalk, gypsum, lead, silica | bauxite, natural gas | phosphates |
| Total Imported | $104.8 billion (1984) foodstuffs, petroleum, machinery, chemicals, crude materials | $8.0 billion (1984) machinery, raw materials | $713 million (1982) foodstuffs, machinery, consumer goods, trans-port equipment |
| Total Exported | $93.7 billion (1984) machinery, transport equipment, chemicals, petroleum, foodstuffs | $8.5 billion (1984) machinery and tools, in-dustrial and consumer goods, raw materials | $476 million (1982) peanuts, phosphate rock, canned fish |
| Major Trading Partners | West Germany, U.S., France, Western Euro-pean countries | U.S.S.R., Warsaw Pact countries, West Ger-many, Yugoslavia, Aus-tria, Italy | France, Western Euro-pean countries, African neighbors |

Sources: *Information Please World Almanac, 1986; The World Almanac and Book of Facts, 1986.*

1. How much trade do you think these three countries have with each other? Use the infor-mation above to support your answer.

_____

2. Which of these three countries needs to trade the most? What information did you use to support your answer?

_____

3. Which country will have the hardest time trading? Does the amount available for trade and the amount of goods imported matter? Explain your answer.

_____

4. How are the availability of natural resources and a nation's wealth related?

_____

# Chapter 18

# What Is a World Region?

**Reading for a Purpose**

1. What is a region?
2. What are the two basic types of regions?
3. Why do people move?
4. What causes urbanization?

## Knowing New Words

geographic region (jee-oh-GRAF-ik REE-jun)   A large area of the earth that is somehow alike.
>   Dianne comes from the highlands, a **geographic region** in Florida.

cultural region (KUL-chuh-rul REE-jun)   A region of the earth where people can be grouped
>   together because of something they have in common.
>   I saw a map of the English-speaking **cultural regions** of the world.

physical region (FIZ-ih-kul REE-jun)   A place on earth where the area is different from other
>   areas around it.
>   The Saudi Arabian desert is an important **physical region** in that part of the world.

migrate (MY-grayt)   To move from one place to another.
>   Birds **migrate** south during the winter.

urbanization (ur-ban-ih-ZAY-shun)   The growth of a large city.
>   The **urbanization** of the valley happened as the capital needed more land.

———————————————— ● ————————————————

    When studying geography you should know how places and the people
who live there are alike and how they are different. The world is divided into
different regions, or areas of the earth that are alike in some way. There are
two basic types of world regions, **physical regions** and **cultural regions**. People
adapt to, or learn to live with, the regions in which they live. People move
themselves and their products from region to region in order to meet their
needs. Some regions have large cities that grow in a process called **urbanization**.

## Writing and Thinking

    Study the cartoon carefully. Then answer the questions on page 101.

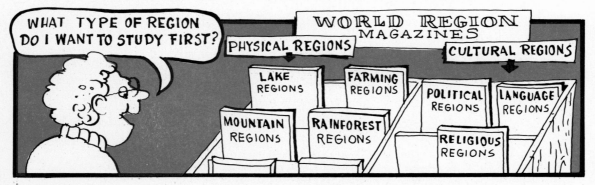

1. What do you think this person wants to read about?

_____

_____

2. What do you think are two basic types of world regions?

_____

3. What do you think a cultural region is? Can you give some examples of cultural regions?

_____

_____

4. What do you think a physical region is? Can you give some examples of physical regions?

_____

_____

5. What are some other types of regions? Are they physical regions or cultural regions?

_____

_____

● After reading this chapter, come back to the answers you have written. Make any changes that you think will make the answer better.

## Geography Skills and Concepts

1. The world is a very large area to study. You have read about landforms, climates, cultures, and other ways in which parts of the world are alike. A **geographic region**, or world region, is a part of the earth in which the area is alike in some way. Studying world regions helps you see how parts of the earth are similar. It also allows geographers to see how the world is different.

2. The world can be divided into many different kinds of regions. The same place could be studied as part of several different regions depending on what you were looking for. One area of the world could be studied to see where people farm and where people in that area do not farm. Or it could be studied to see where there were mountains, warm spots, or dry areas. But there are two basic geographic regions—cultural regions and physical regions. Cultural regions are areas of the earth where people can be put into groups because they have something in common that makes them different from other groups. Physical regions are areas of the earth that are different from the areas that surround them. If you were studying a farm area, you would be studying a farming region. If you were studying a region that was mountainous, you would be studying a mountain region.

*Terraced rice fields in China; a synagogue; mountains in Switzerland. Which photographs show examples of physical regions?*

**3.** What can be learned by studying world regions? Studying the world by regions allows you to see how it is both alike and different. The study of world regions tells you how people adapt, or learn to live with, the area in which they live. A map of how people in the world make a living will show that people in Japan, Greenland, and Portugal are alike. The way in which they are alike is that many of the people in these places fish for a living. A temperature map will show that the people in the same three countries live in different climate regions.

**4.** The people in a given region may be alike or different depending on their way of life. Their way of life comes from the way in which they have adapted to their environment. Different people will choose to use their environment differently. This is often true even if their physical environments are alike. By studying world regions on maps, the differences and similarities can be understood.

**5.** Throughout the ages people have moved. But why do they move? Sometimes it is a matter of moving within their own region. At other times people will move from one region to another. People move for basically one reason. They want to improve their way of life. They may make the move to improve the way the government treats them, to make more money, or to feel safer. When people move from one place to another, we say that they are **migrating**.

**6.** The United States is a good place to study regions. You may have heard people talk about the sunbelt region and the snowbelt region in the United States. One difference between the two regions is the number of people who live in each. Years ago people would migrate from the South to the North, causing the snowbelt to grow. There were lots of factories in the North, so it was a manufacturing region. Where there were factories, towns grew. As one factory grew, other manufacturers came to the area and the town grew. The growth of the cities they made is called urbanization.

**7.** Today lots of people are migrating south to the Sunbelt. Other people are moving there from the Spanish-speaking countries of Central and South America. One of the reasons that people are moving to the Sunbelt is that they like the warm weather. With the invention of air conditioning, technology has made life in warm areas easier. A region that was too warm for many people has now become a place where people prefer to live.

## Understanding What You Have Read

Choose the word or words that best complete each statement. Write the letter of your answer in the blank next to the number.

_____ 1. Moving from one country to another is called
   a. migration   b. urbanization   c. region

_____ 2. When people in a particular area share a common language it is called a
   a. physical region   b. region   c. cultural region

_____ 3. When an area has a common landform that makes it different from other areas it is called a
   a. physical region   b. region   c. cultural region

_____ 4. The tallest mountains in the world are in the Himalayas, which is a
   a. plateau region   b. mountain-range region   c. rain-forest region

_____ 5. World-famous tulips are grown in South Holland, a province of the Netherlands. The people there speak Dutch, and the area is known for its windmills. In studying a map of language regions for South Holland, you would expect to find a label or symbol for
   a. tulips   b. Dutch   c. windmills

_____ 6. Vermont is famous for having more cows than people. Therefore, you could say that Vermont is a
   a. cultural region   b. manufacturing region   c. farming region

_____ 7. Growing rice takes a lot of water and full sun. Southeastern China grows a lot of rice. Therefore, southeastern China is probably a
   a. rain-forest region   b. heavy rainfall region   c. desert region

_____ 8. There are free and democratic governments in Canada and Sweden. The Soviet Union has a Communist government. To show these countries as different on a world map, the type of region you would show is a
   a. political region   b. physical region   c. geographic region

## Classifying

List the different physical and cultural regions into which the world can be divided.

| Physical Regions | Cultural Regions |
|---|---|
|  |  |

## Essay

Talk to someone in your family or to a person you know who has emigrated or migrated. Find out what country or place this person has moved from and why. Write a brief essay that explains why the person moved. Use the information in this chapter.

# Unit 5 Review

## Reading Maps

Study the maps. Do you agree or disagree with the statements below? Briefly explain your reasons for agreeing or disagreeing. Use the maps to support your opinions.

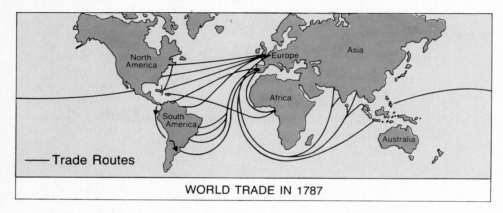

WORLD TRADE IN 1787

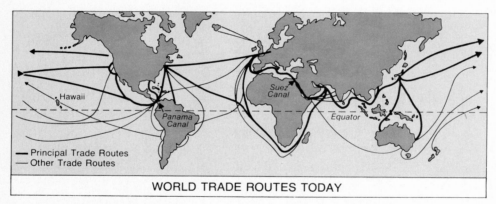

WORLD TRADE ROUTES TODAY

1. There is little sharing of products and ideas among countries of the world.

_____

_____

2. Trade among countries has changed a great deal since 1787.

_____

_____

3. The Suez and Panama canals have helped to bring about more trade among countries.

_____

_____

4. The world today can be called a shrinking world.

_____

_____

5. All nations must trade.

_____

6. There is more cultural diffusion today than there was in 1787.

_____

_____

7. Countries of the world depend upon each other.

_____

_____

8. The United States trades more with some parts of the world than with others.

_____

_____

9. The maps show that people throughout the world are interdependent.

_____

_____

10. Internationalism has grown since 1787.

_____

_____

_____

## Reading for the Main Idea

Read the paragraphs below. Then study the picture on page 106. Color in only those items in the picture that are in your life as a result of cultural diffusion. What does this tell you about cultural diffusion and your way of life?

### What We Owe to Others

We think of ourselves as Americans. Most of us are proud of what we own. We usually feel good when we give things to other people who are not as well off as we are. Few of us, however, realize how much we owe to other people. Take, for example, the plants and animals that we eat as food. Some of these came from Europe. We took corn, beans, squash, potatoes, and tobacco from the American Indians (Native Americans). The Chinese taught us about paper making. We learned about soap and the compass from the Arabs. Our seven-day week started with the Babylonians. Our alphabet started with the Phoenicians of western Asia. Our popular music has some of its roots in Latin America and Africa.

Every day there are reminders of how our good life was given to us by others. You may wake up in the morning in a bed like the one first thought of in the Middle East. You then may put your feet down on a rug like those first made in Asia. You take a bath in a tub similar to those made years ago in the Middle East. Later, you might eat on dishes like those first made in China. All this happens in a house made with cement, which was invented by an Englishman. You might ride to school on a bicycle. This, too, was given to the world by an English inventor.

Color in only those items in the picture that are a result of cultural diffusion.

# GEOGRAPHY HIGHLIGHTS

## Continent Size

■ Which continent is largest and which is smallest? Land covers only 29 percent of the earth's surface. This chart shows the area of each continent in millions of square miles. It also shows the percentage of the earth's land surface that each covers.

| Continent | Millions of Square Miles | Percentage of Earth's Land Surface |
|---|---|---|
| Asia | 16.9 | 29.4 |
| Africa | 11.5 | 20.0 |
| North America | 8.4 | 14.7 |
| South America | 6.8 | 11.8 |
| Antarctica | 5.5 | 9.5 |
| Europe | 3.8 | 5.1 |
| Australia | 2.9 | 5.1 |

# The Atlas

## Reading for a Purpose

Why do we use maps?

## Geography Skills and Concepts

1. There are many uses for maps. One important use is to help you find out more about people. A skilled map reader can learn many things about the geography in which people live by looking at a map. Such a person can also use maps to learn about people's culture.

2. On the following pages are maps of regions around the world. You can use these maps to find out about people. You will also need to use your skill and knowledge of geography. By answering the questions you will learn a great deal about the people living in each region.

## Writing and Thinking

Study the cartoon. Then answer the questions that follow.

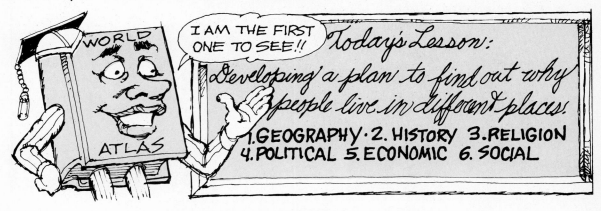

1. What is meant by the title on the chalkboard?

_____

_____

2. What is an atlas?

_____

3. Why is the teacher of the class shown as an atlas?

_____

4. What are three ways that maps can tell you about the people living in a place?

_____

_____

_____

## NORTH AMERICA

Use the maps on both pages to help you find answers to the questions.

1. Is this region north or south of the equator?

_____

2. Is this region east or west of the prime meridian?

_____

_____

3. How might the region's latitude affect the way people live there?

_____

_____

_____

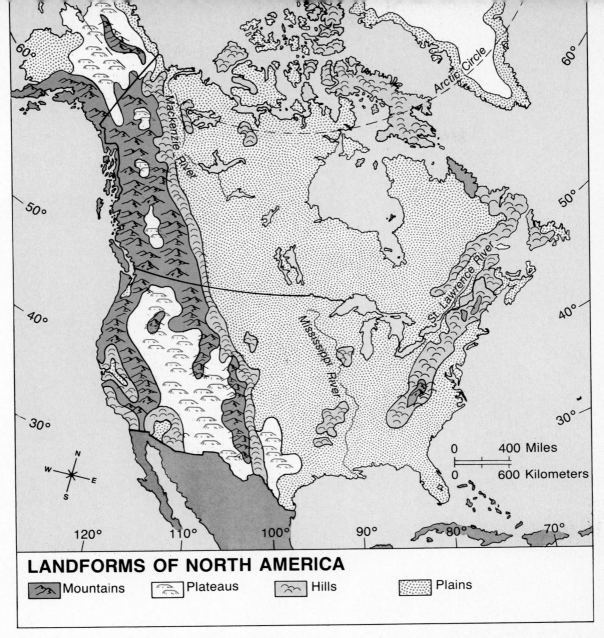

## LANDFORMS OF NORTH AMERICA

Mountains    Plateaus    Hills    Plains

4. If there are any large mountain ranges on the topographic map, give their locations. (Use latitude and longitude in your answer.)

_____

_____

5. How might mountain ranges affect the lives of people in the region? Will everyone be affected equally?

_____

_____

6. What other topographic features can you find in this region?

7. How might these topographic features affect people living near them?

_____

_____

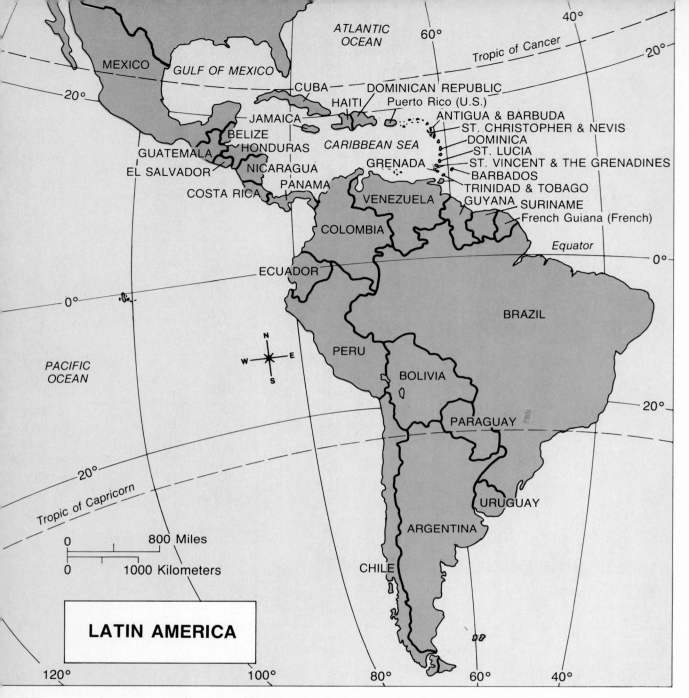

LATIN AMERICA

Use the maps on both pages to help you find answers to the questions.

1. Is this region in the low, middle, or high latitudes?

_____

2. How many miles north and south does the region extend?

_____

3. What does the map tell you about the size of the region as a whole and the size of individual countries?

_____

_____

_____

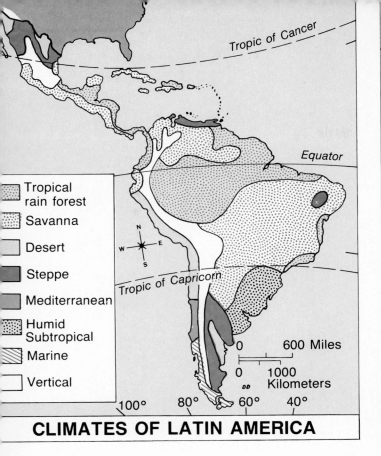

**CLIMATES OF LATIN AMERICA**

Tropic of Cancer

Equator

Tropic of Capricorn

Tropical rain forest

Savanna

Desert

Steppe

Mediterranean

Humid Subtropical

Marine

Vertical

0          600 Miles

0     1000 Kilometers

100°    80°    60°    40°

**NATURAL RESOURCES OF LATIN AMERICA**

Tropic of Cancer

Equator

Tropic of Capricorn

B  Bauxite
C  Coal
O  Oil
X  Natural Gas
+  Copper
I  Iron
D  Diamonds
M  Manganese
G  Gold
T  Tin
U  Uranium

600  Miles

400 Kilometers

100°    80°    60°    40°

4. Name five major natural resources found in the region and tell where they are located.

_____

_____

_____

_____

5. How might the natural resources in a region affect the people living there?

_____

_____

_____

6. Name the different climate zones in the region.

_____

_____

_____

7. How might the climate affect the people living in the region?

_____

_____

_____

**111**

**EUROPE**

Use the maps on both pages to help you find answers to the questions.

1. How many miles east and west does the region extend?

_____

2. List two ways in which the location of the region might affect the lives of the people. For example, how would trade with other countries of the world be affected?

_____

_____

_____

3. Name the chief bodies of water that border the region.

_____

_____

112

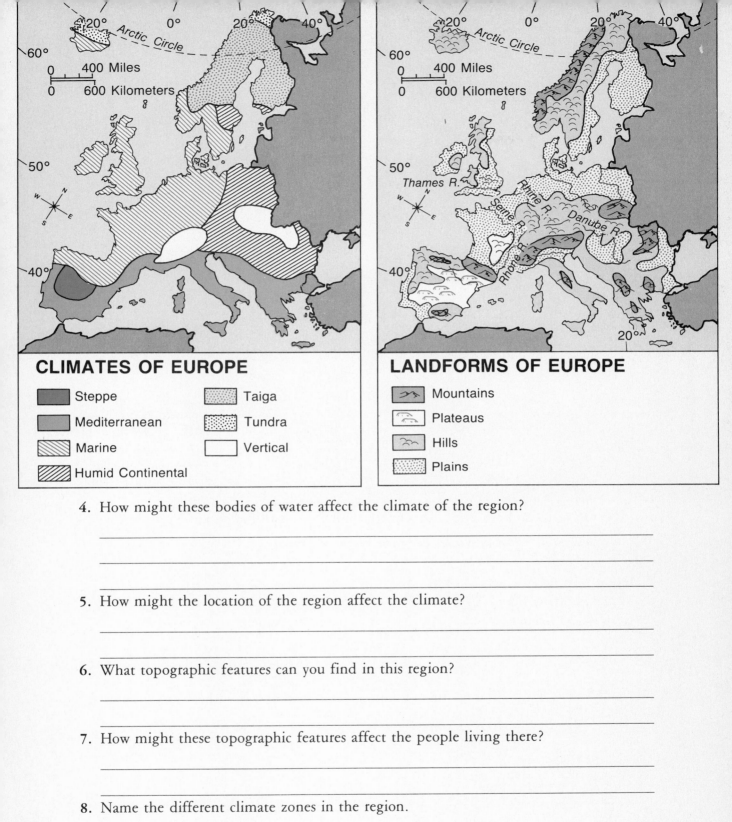

## CLIMATES OF EUROPE

- Steppe
- Mediterranean
- Marine
- Humid Continental
- Taiga
- Tundra
- Vertical

## LANDFORMS OF EUROPE

- Mountains
- Plateaus
- Hills
- Plains

4. How might these bodies of water affect the climate of the region?

_____

_____

5. How might the location of the region affect the climate?

_____

6. What topographic features can you find in this region?

_____

7. How might these topographic features affect the people living there?

_____

8. Name the different climate zones in the region.

_____

_____

9. If there are countries in this region that have no coastlines, name them.

_____

_____

Use the maps on both pages to help you find answers to the questions.

1. How many miles east and west does the region extend?

   _____

2. List at least two ways in which the size and location of the region might affect the lives of people living there?

   _____

   _____

   _____

3. Name five major natural resources found in the region and tell where each is located.

   _____

   _____

   _____

   _____

   _____

4. How might the type of natural resource in an area affect the people living there?

   _____

   _____

   _____

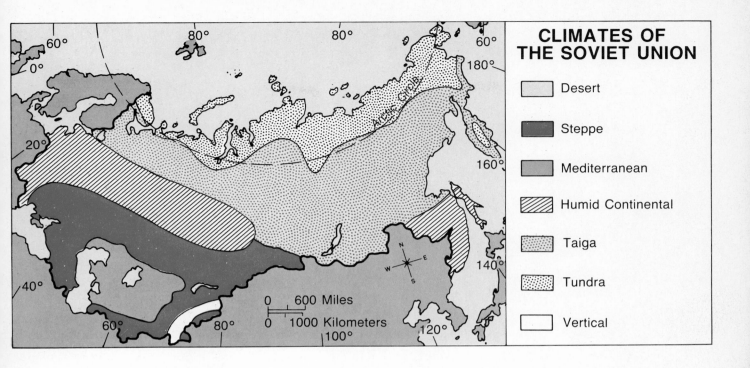

## CLIMATES OF THE SOVIET UNION

- Desert
- Steppe
- Mediterranean
- Humid Continental
- Taiga
- Tundra
- Vertical

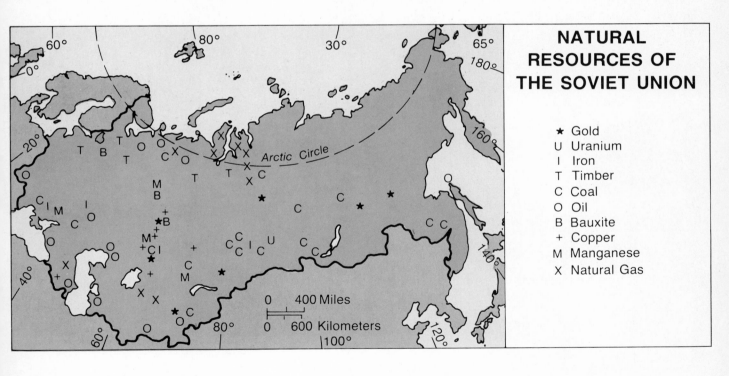

## NATURAL RESOURCES OF THE SOVIET UNION

- ★ Gold
- U Uranium
- I Iron
- T Timber
- C Coal
- O Oil
- B Bauxite
- + Copper
- M Manganese
- X Natural Gas

5. Name the different climate zones in the region.

_____

_____

6. How might climate affect the way people live in different parts of the region?

_____

_____

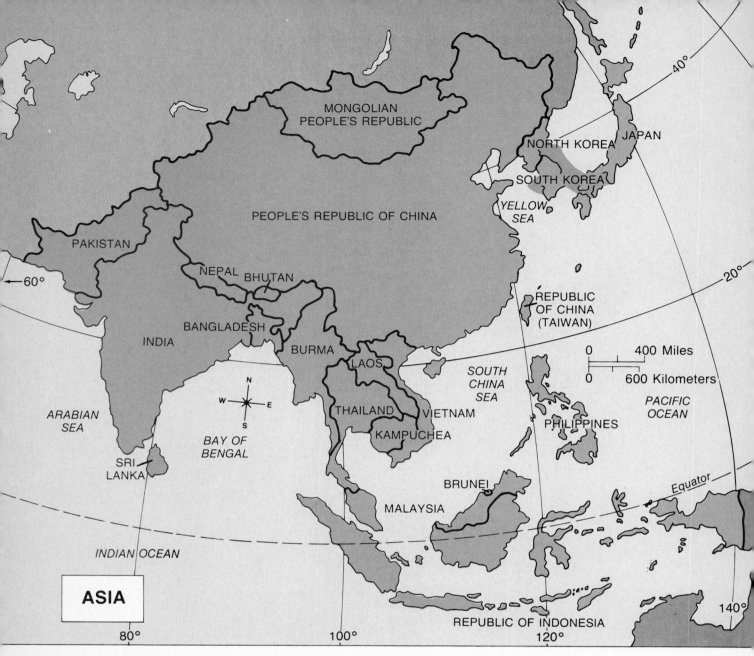

Use the maps on both pages to help you find answers to the questions.

1. Is this region north or south of the equator?

_____

2. Is this region in the low, middle, or high latitudes?

_____

3. Name three countries in this region that are completely surrounded by water.

_____

4. Which country in the region has the largest land area?

_____

_____

_____

_____

116

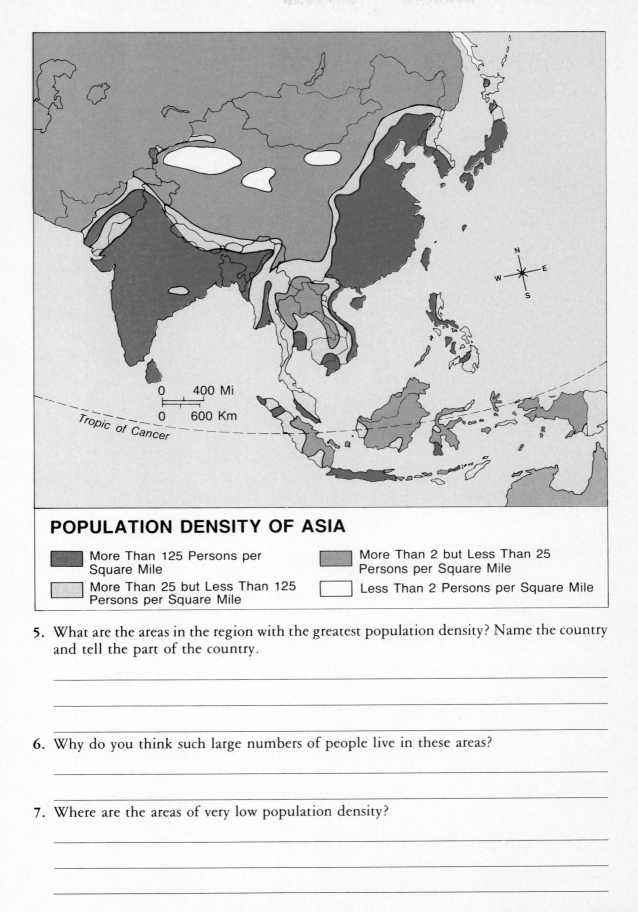

## POPULATION DENSITY OF ASIA

More Than 125 Persons per Square Mile

More Than 25 but Less Than 125 Persons per Square Mile

More Than 2 but Less Than 25 Persons per Square Mile

Less Than 2 Persons per Square Mile

0     400 Mi

0     600 Km

*Tropic of Cancer*

5. What are the areas in the region with the greatest population density? Name the country and tell the part of the country.

_____

_____

_____

6. Why do you think such large numbers of people live in these areas?

_____

_____

7. Where are the areas of very low population density?

_____

_____

_____

# NORTH AFRICA AND THE MIDDLE EAST

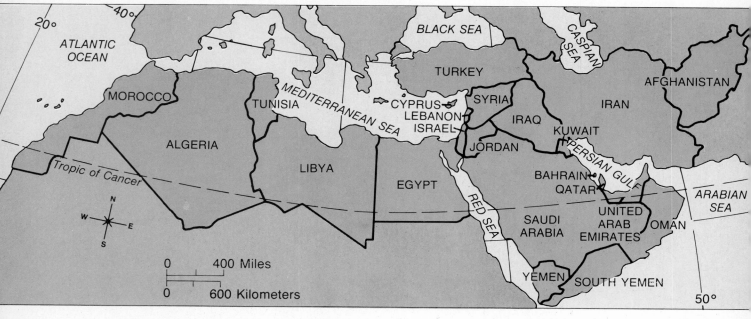

Use the maps on both pages to help you find answers to the questions.

1. Is this region north or south of the equator?

   _____

2. How might the region's latitude affect the lives of people living there? (Use the climate
   and population density maps to help you answer the question.)

   _____

   _____

3. What are the chief bodies of water that border the region?

   _____

   _____

   _____

4. How might these bodies of water affect the lives of the people?

   _____

   _____

   _____

5. Name the different climate zones in the region.

   _____

   _____

6. How might the climate affect the people in the region?

   _____

   _____

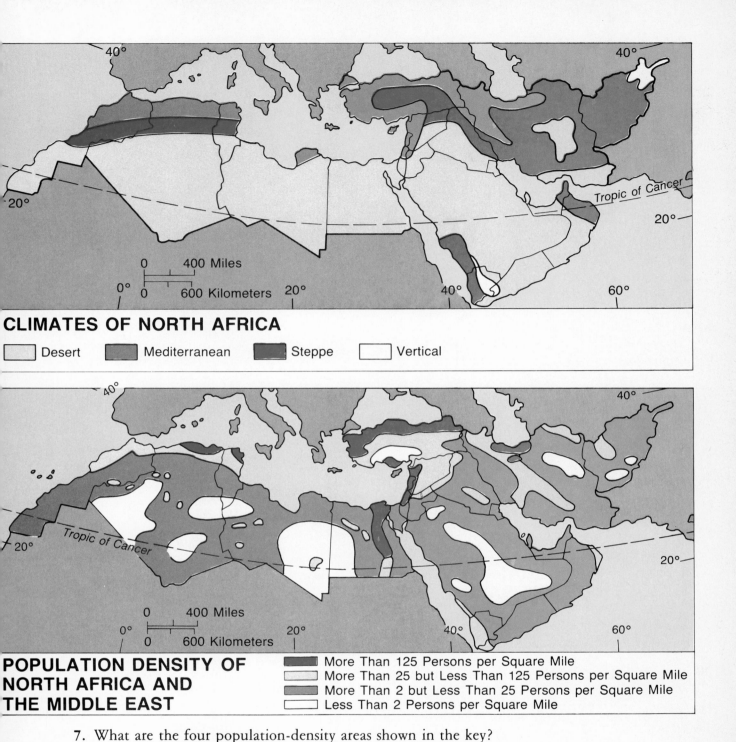

## CLIMATES OF NORTH AFRICA

| | | | | | | | |
|---|---|---|---|---|---|---|---|
| ▢ Desert | ▨ Mediterranean | ▧ Steppe | ▢ Vertical | | | | |

## POPULATION DENSITY OF
## NORTH AFRICA AND
## THE MIDDLE EAST

▨ More Than 125 Persons per Square Mile
▢ More Than 25 but Less Than 125 Persons per Square Mile
▧ More Than 2 but Less Than 25 Persons per Square Mile
▢ Less Than 2 Persons per Square Mile

7. What are the four population-density areas shown in the key?

_____

_____

8. What connection do you see between climate areas and population density? (Compare the two maps.)

_____

_____

_____

119

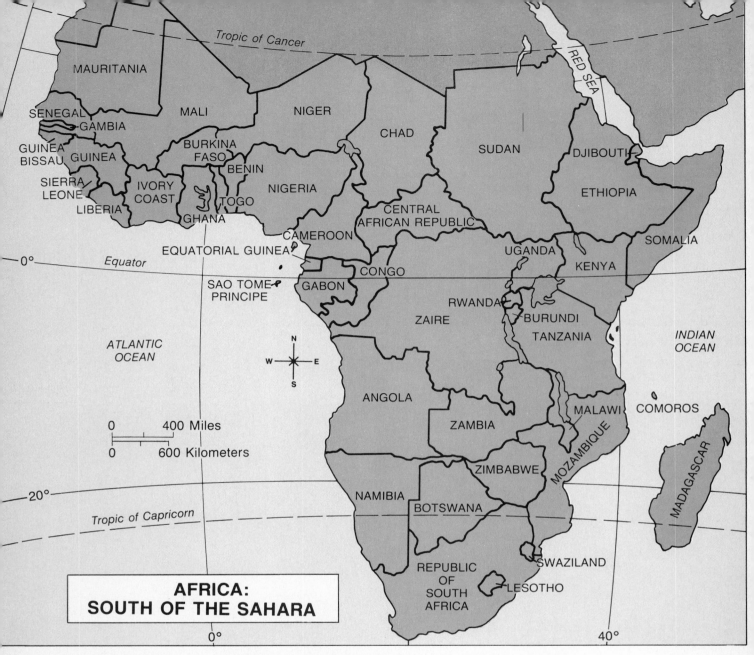

**AFRICA: SOUTH OF THE SAHARA**

Use the maps on both pages to help you find answers to the questions.

1. Is this region east or west of the prime meridian?

_____

2. How might the region's latitude affect the way people live there?

_____

_____

3. Name five major natural resources found in the area and tell where they are located.

_____

_____

_____

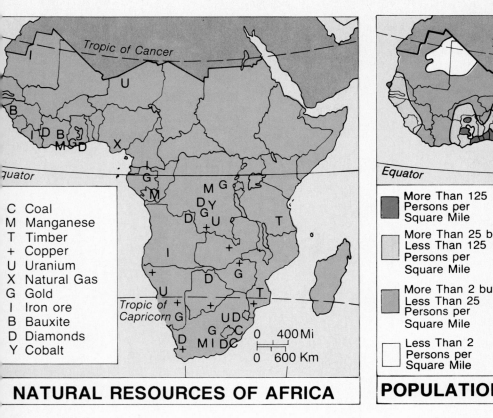

C Coal
M Manganese
T Timber
+ Copper
U Uranium
X Natural Gas
G Gold
I Iron ore
B Bauxite
D Diamonds
Y Cobalt

**NATURAL RESOURCES OF AFRICA**

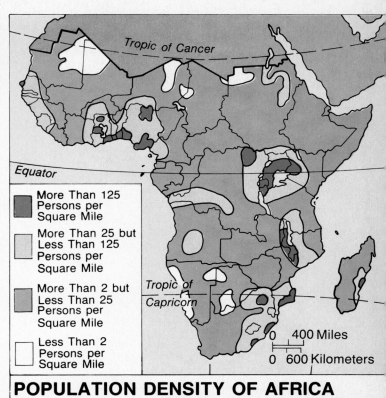

More Than 125
Persons per
Square Mile

More Than 25 but
Less Than 125
Persons per
Square Mile

More Than 2 but
Less Than 25
Persons per
Square Mile

Less Than 2
Persons per
Square Mile

**POPULATION DENSITY OF AFRICA**

4. How might the presence of natural resources affect where people live? (Compare the political map and the population density map.)

5. Name the five areas of greatest population density.

6. Why do you think such large numbers of people live in these areas? (Use the population density and natural resources maps.)

7. Name areas of very low population density.

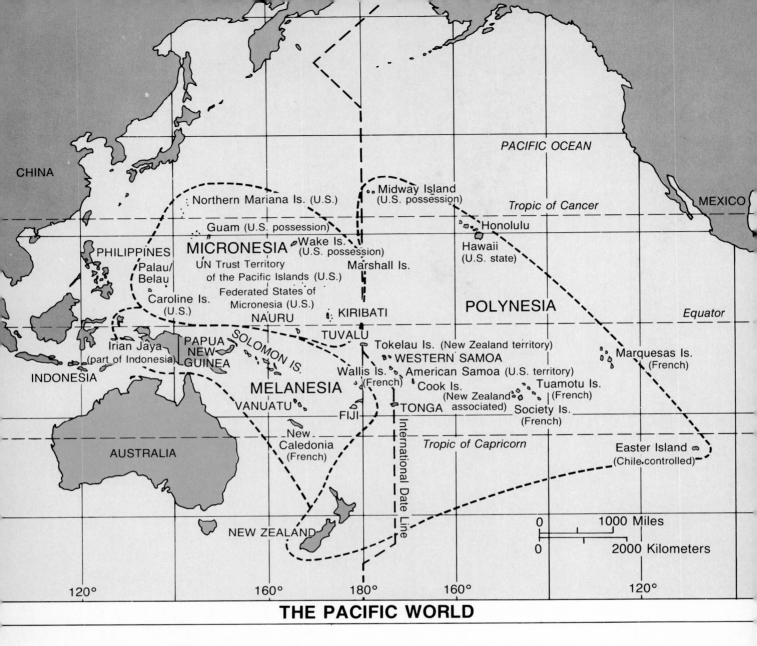

CHINA

PHILIPPINES

INDONESIA

AUSTRALIA

PACIFIC OCEAN

MEXICO

Northern Mariana Is. (U.S.)

Midway Island
(U.S. possession)

Tropic of Cancer

Guam (U.S. possession)

Honolulu

MICRONESIA

Wake Is.
(U.S. possession)

Hawaii
(U.S. state)

Palau/
Belau

UN Trust Territory
of the Pacific Islands (U.S.)

Marshall Is.

Caroline Is.
(U.S.)

Federated States of
Micronesia (U.S.)

POLYNESIA

Equator

NAURU

KIRIBATI

TUVALU

Irian Jaya
(part of Indonesia)

PAPUA
NEW
GUINEA

SOLOMON IS.

Tokelau Is. (New Zealand territory)

Marquesas Is.
(French)

WESTERN SAMOA

Wallis Is.
(French)

American Samoa (U.S. territory)

MELANESIA

Cook Is.
(New Zealand
associated)

Tuamotu Is.
(French)

VANUATU

FIJI

TONGA

Society Is.
(French)

New
Caledonia
(French)

Tropic of Capricorn

Easter Island
(Chile controlled)

International Date Line

0        1000 Miles

0        2000 Kilometers

NEW ZEALAND

120°          160°          180°          160°          120°

**THE PACIFIC WORLD**

Use the maps on both pages to help you find answers to the questions.

1. Is this region in the low, middle, or high latitudes? _____

2. Name any countries that are islands or groups of islands.

_____

_____

3. How might the region's latitude affect the ways that people live there?

_____

_____

4. Name major natural resources and tell how they may affect the way people live in Australia and New Zealand.

_____

_____

122

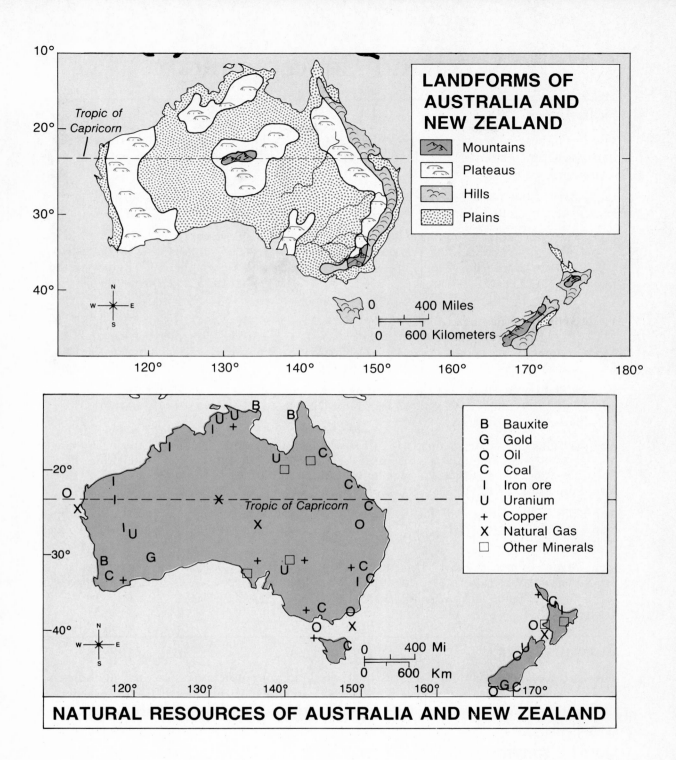

## LANDFORMS OF AUSTRALIA AND NEW ZEALAND

Mountains
Plateaus
Hills
Plains

Tropic of Capricorn

0   400 Miles
0   600 Kilometers

### NATURAL RESOURCES OF AUSTRALIA AND NEW ZEALAND

B   Bauxite
G   Gold
O   Oil
C   Coal
I   Iron ore
U   Uranium
+   Copper
X   Natural Gas
☐   Other Minerals

Tropic of Capricorn

0   400 Mi
0   600 Km

5. How might landforms and water forms affect the way people live in those countries?

# Skills and Concepts Index

## Skills Index

The list indicates exercises in which the skills are developed or used. Circle those skills that you wish to strengthen. Then go back to the pages listed next to the skill and review that material.

**Vocabulary Skills** Knowing New Words, 1, 6, 10, 15, 23, 29, 36, 41, 48, 51, 56, 66, 71, 75, 80, 89, 94, 100; Building Your Vocabulary, 4, 21, 33, 45, 85

**Comprehension Skills** Using What You Know (includes Unit Reviews), 21–22, 45–47, 62–65, 85–88, 93, 98; Understanding What You Have Read, 4–5, 22, 27, 39, 44, 46, 50, 55, 60–61, 69, 78, 103; Living Your Geography, 64–65; Thinking with Geography, 39; Reviewing the Facts, 2–3, 7–8, 11–12, 16–18, 24–27, 30–32, 37–39, 42–43, 49–50, 53–54, 58–60, 68–69, 72–73, 76–77, 81–82, 90–91, 95–96, 101–102

**Visual Skills** Interpreting Cartoons, 2, 6, 15, 23–24, 29–30, 36–37, 41, 48–49, 75, 81, 83, 90, 94–95, 100–101; Interpreting Charts, 43, 57, 65, 78, 86–87, 99; Interpreting Diagrams, 42, 51, 56; Interpreting Photos, 7, 8, 31, 32, 57, 67, 97; Interpreting Pictographs, 80–81; Interpreting Puzzles, 71–72

**Writing Skills** 55, 79, 80, 83, 84; Writing and Thinking, 2, 6–7, 10–11, 15–16, 23–24, 29–30, 36–37, 41, 48–49, 51–53, 57, 66–67, 71–72, 75, 80–81, 89–90, 94–95, 100–101, 104–105; Writing an Essay, 70, 103

**Analytic Skills** 5; Categorizing, 74; Classifying, 103; Comparing, 8–9; Critical Thinking, 69, 78, 86–87; Distinguishing True and False Statements, 27, 55, 91–92, 97; Getting the Main Idea, 80–81, 83, 105–106; Making Inferences, 64, 70, 86–87; Outlining, 61; Reading for a Purpose, 1, 6, 10, 15, 23, 29, 36, 41, 48, 51, 56, 66, 71, 75, 80, 89, 94, 100, 107

**Map Skills** Completing and Making Maps, 14, 55; Reading, Interpreting, and Understanding Maps, 2–3, 7, 8–9, 10–11, 12, 13, 17–18, 23–24, 25–26, 39, 47, 51–53, 62–63, 87–88, 92–93, 104–105, 108–123

**Using Maps** Climate, 62–63; Directions, 9, 13; Identifying Continents, 28; Identifying Landforms and Waterforms, 35; Identifying Map Projections, 25–27, 28; Identifying Places, 18, 22, 47; Latitude and Longitude, 19–20, 22, 57–60; Locating Places, 9; Topography, 34, 47

---

## Concepts Index

The list indicates the major concepts developed. In your notebook, list each of these items. Then write all the important ideas you can think of that are related to each of these concepts. When you are done, check your ideas with those presented in each chapter.

**Chapter 1:** geography, globe, map  **Chapter 2:** chart, chartographer, compass rose  **Chapter 3:** legend or key, scale  **Chapter 4:** latitude, longitude  **Chapter 5:** map distortion, map projections, (conic, cylinder, plane) hemispheres  **Chapter 6:** landforms, population location  **Chapter 7:** effects of earth's spinning on ocean currents and airflow  **Chapter 8:** source of rainfall, river formation  **Chapter 9:** climate and its effects on people  **Chapter 10:** factors that affect climate  **Chapter 11:** climate zones based on latitude, climate's effect on population location  **Chapter 12:** culture, basic human needs, technology and environment, geographical location and spread of culture, ethnocentrism  **Chapter 13:** natural resources  **Chapter 14:** cities and their origin, people's response to natural environment  **Chapter 15:** effects of technology, Industrial Revolution  **Chapter 16:** value of natural resources  **Chapter 17:** cultural diffusion, interdependence, world political divisions  **Chapter 18:** physical and cultural regions, adaptation to regions, urbanization